ORIGINS OF ARABIA

ANDREW THOMPSON

STACEY INTERNATIONAL
LONDON

ORIGINS OF ARABIA

ANDREW THOMPSON

ACKNOWLEDGEMENTS

Many people along the way have contributed to this book. Ideas and thoughts from many books and articles have informed me; suggestions from and discussions with friends have guided me in interesting directions. To list all those involved is impossible, but to select a few is invidious. Nonetheless, some deserve to be mentioned particularly.

Peter Lenthall, Vernon and Jeanne Cassin, John and Susie Pint, Ken and Patricia Palmer, and Peter and Patricia Barbor all took me to places I would not otherwise have known of or seen; I took pleasure in their company and learnt much from them.

Colin Edwards did me a great service in giving me much interesting material on the geology of the peninsula; Terry Adams, Abdulaziz Laboun and Fay and Kevin Dunham were also inspirational.

Addie Carpenter took the photograph on page 80, in the course of a memorable journey to the Jibal Wajid.

Tom Stacey has been my taskmaster. Critical in the best sense, occasionally severe, he has patiently coaxed and encouraged me in the process of writing the book. He, Mela and Mark all have my thanks, as does especially my wife Ionis, who also did not lose faith that the book would eventually see the light of day.

A.T.

© Stacey International and Andrew Thompson 2000

Project Managers: Mark Petre, Kitty Carruthers
Editor: Mela Davidson
Designers: Frank Ainscough, Mark Petre
Graphics: David A. Hardy
All photographs by Andrew Thompson except: Addie Carpenter (top, p. 81), Planet Earth (bottom, p. 23),
Rex Features, London (top, p. 84)
Filmset and colour reproduction by Aurora Press, Croydon, England

Printed and bound by Oriental Press, Dubai.

British Cataloguing in Publication Data.
A catalogue record for this book is available from the British Library.

ISBN 1 900988 04 6

Stacey International
128 Kensington Church Street
London W8 4BH
Fax: 020 7792 9288
E-mail: stacey_international@compuserve.com

CONTENTS

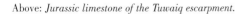

Above: *Jurassic limestone of the Tuwaiq escarpment.*

Opposite title: *As the Tuwaiq escarpment marches south the uniform limestone thicknesses in the Riyadh area change to a more mixed sequence of rock types. Jebel Baloum, in the photograph, is an outlier from the main escarpment west of Hawtah. Sandstone at its lower levels mixed with conglomerate and shale, give way towards the summit to a white limestone.*

INTRODUCTION

This book grew out of a search for the answers to many questions that presented themselves as I travelled about Arabia. Questions about the landscape, questions about the fossils on the desert surface, questions of all sorts to which no satisfactory explanations were readily accessible.

The world, the ground under our feet, we take to be unchanging. In fact, given a long enough perspective, it is very far from changeless. Continents swing around the globe, colliding with each other; oceans widen and narrow; land rises and falls. The same spot may in past ages have seen glaciers and rain forests, coral reefs and dry desert.

This book presents such a picture of Arabia. It describes the first origins and subsequent adventures of the Arabian peninsula, taking the story down to recent times. It gives a basic explanation of some of the geological principles and forces behind these changes, and weaves in the fossil record and the changing climate in building up the picture.

As the story reaches more recent times, the arrival of man and his relation with the rocks, the water resources and the useful minerals of the land are described. Much has been compressed into a small volume. The tale is told as a chronology, and written for the intelligent layman who travels in Arabia and looks for answers to the questions about the land which naturally come to his mind.

In hunting for the answers I found no shortage of source material. A truly remarkable quantity of geological exploration, analysis and detective work has been published over the last fifty years, nearly all of which has been written by geologists for geologists and is, unfortunately for the layman, written in the highly technical language of the scientist. There are also impressive archives of work on natural history and palaeontology – testimony to the learning and labour of many scientists in those and related fields. I pay tribute to them here. My hope is that this book, Origins of Arabia, will make the reader more familiar and more comfortable with the land in which he travels, and open his eyes to some of the many marvels it contains.

A.T.

CHAPTER ONE

ARABIAN ORIGINS

SURFACE GEOLOGY OF ARABIA

The peninsula is divided into several main geological provinces. The western half is dominated by the Arabian Shield, an assemblage of different igneous and metamorphic rocks which together are the oldest in Arabia. To the east lies a series of sedimentary rock regions, becoming progressively younger towards the Arabian Gulf. Sand, coastal sediments, and the extensive basalt sheets of the harrats (lava fields) cover wide areas of these two main provinces. Oman, which went through very different geological processes in its formation, has a band of old ocean bed, called ophiolite, prominent in its surface rocks.

A billion years ago there was no land to the north east of Africa for many hundreds of kilometres, except for a long chain of volcanic islands far offshore, recently emerged from the sea. These islands were entirely barren: no grass or trees covered their slopes, no living creature inhabited them; 500 million more years were to pass before the first living things began to invade the land from the sea. This volcanic wilderness, strung across the sea rather as Indonesia is today, was the first sign of the land that was eventually to form Arabia.

But long even before then the Earth was already old. The best scientific estimate of the age of the earth and the other planets of the solar system is about four and a half billion years, based on radiometric analysis of lead and uranium isotopes in meteorites and in moon rock brought back by astronauts. This dating would fit comfortably with the age of the most ancient rocks so far found on earth. These are grains of zircon, 3.8 billion years old, found in Australia. Other rocks almost as old have been found in Greenland and South Africa. The context in which these rocks were laid down has shown that

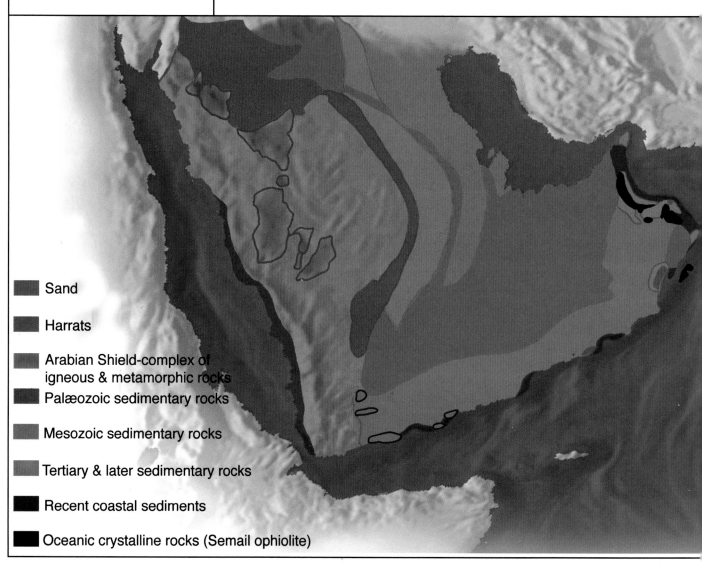

- Sand
- Harrats
- Arabian Shield-complex of igneous & metamorphic rocks
- Palæozoic sedimentary rocks
- Mesozoic sedimentary rocks
- Tertiary & later sedimentary rocks
- Recent coastal sediments
- Oceanic crystalline rocks (Semail ophiolite)

volcanic processes and rainwater erosion played a part in creating them, so we may deduce that the world's oceans, some of its continents, and its weather systems were all present very soon after the earth was first created.

The earliest life to colonise the seas of this first sterile world were microscopic single-celled bacteria. They are thought to have emerged over three billion years ago, splitting into many distinct bacterial species to fill different ecological gaps. Some surface dwellers used energy from sunlight to grow and multiply, giving off oxygen in the process; these were the earliest photosynthesisers. Others living deeper in the water oxidised sulphur and were not dependent on sunlight. The many forms coexisted as mats of green slime or scum which hardly looked like living organisms, but which as time progressed concealed a vast diversity of microscopic forms and functions. These creatures left very little fossil record, being in the main too small and soft bodied to be preserved. Strange columns of mudstone called stromatolites are preserved in ancient rock. They represent silt trapped in mats of primitive algae. As the algae became smothered with silt they formed a new colony above the silt, reaching for the sunlight. Repeated countless times, this process resulted in the silt building up into columns; of the algae almost no trace remains. Some of these strange "fossils" date back over three billion years.

Less tangible but much more important was the role these first life forms played in making the earth habitable for us. The earth's atmosphere and seas in those earliest days contained almost no free oxygen. The efficient aerobic respiration and metabolism which we and all other higher forms of life employ could not evolve. Very gradually, over the immense space of more than two billion years when bacteria and algae were the sole inhabitants of the earth, the oxygen generated by their photosynthetic activity increased atmospheric oxygen up to its present level of 21 per cent, a level sufficient to support aerobic respiration and metabolism. The level rose much more sharply towards the end of the period. At first, the ferrous iron in the world's oceans captured all the oxygen produced, forming ferric oxides. It has been concisely said that that was the age when the world rusted. Only when that process was complete did free oxygen levels increase. By 1.8 billion years ago, oxygen levels had risen, but still made up only one per cent of the world's atmosphere. At a quickening pace, by a billion years ago, at the time the first Arabian land appeared above the sea, increasing oxygen levels had changed the seas and the atmosphere to a condition that was close to being able to support complex life-forms; yet still the seas around the volcanic archipelago lying off northeast Africa would have contained only bacteria, algal slime and a few primitive jellyfish and annelid worms.

By 600 million years ago, when life did start greatly to diversify and flourish, oxygen levels were almost like today's. By that time the structure of the Arabian peninsula had essentially been formed. Great geological forces were to change its surface many times thereafter, but the basic structure was in place.

In telling the story of Arabia's development we will not be able to avoid the geological time scale. It has been said that people are able to comprehend reasonably well a time span of five generations from grandparent to grandchild, roughly a century. Beyond that, time becomes increasingly difficult to grasp. Geologists use multiples of a million years as the minimum useful time period. We must do the same; but let us think of that million year unit as ten thousand centuries, and we will better understand the immensity of geological time. It is difficult to describe the events which ended with the creation of today's Arabian peninsula without giving a misleading impression of speed. The fact is that most geological developments then were gradual and piecemeal, as they are today. An observer down the ages would probably not have witnessed much difference in the violence or the speed of the geological processes at that ancient time from that which we see now. Our present earth is changing too, but it is hard for us to see the pattern because the changes over a lifetime seem small and inconsequential.

Those first volcanic islands, which geologists now refer to as the Asir island-arc, were thrust out of the sea by the collision of two small tectonic plates. How this process works is interesting, but to understand it we need to step back and look at the causes of movement in the earth's crust.

At depths greater than 100 kilometres the minerals in the earth's mantle are subjected to such great heat and pressure that they are in a perpetually liquid

ARABIA'S PLATE TECTONIC SETTING

The Arabian plate is moving very gradually northeastwards, separating from the African plate along the line of the Red Sea and Gulf of Aden. The force of the collision with the Eurasian plate has resulted in the formation of the Zagros Mountain, Iran.

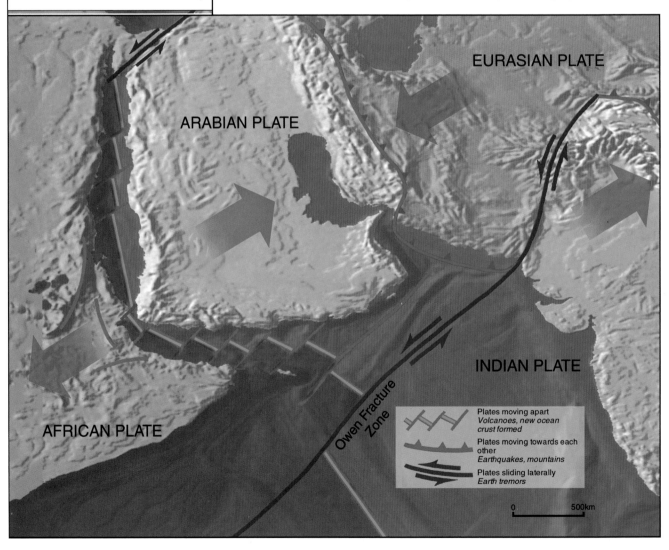

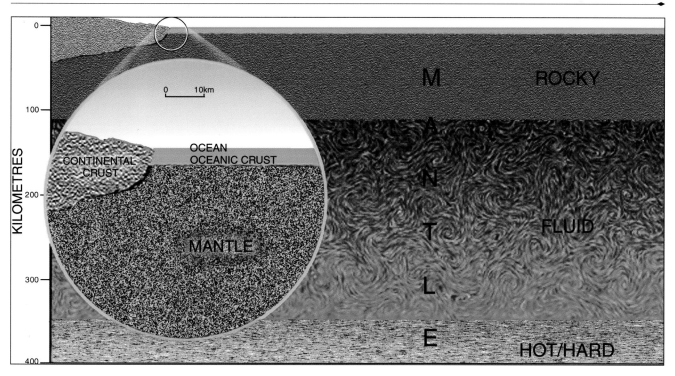

and plastic form, a form which we only see occasionally on the surface as volcanic lava and magma. It is now realised that the hard, rocky outer crust of the earth can and does move over this liquid mantle, carried by vast convection currents in the liquid interior of the earth.

But these movements are not uniform. The crust is pulled and pushed in different directions, and is consequently broken into large segments called tectonic plates. There are six large and a dozen smaller plates which cover the earth's surface, moving in varying directions at rates of between 2 and 12 centimetres a year. Where two plates move apart as is happening now in the Red Sea (see pages xx) hot liquid magma rises from the mantle to fill the gap between them, cooling as it reaches the sea bed to form new rock. In places where two plates are pushed together, the collision will have one of two results. If both colliding edges are continental land masses they will force up a high folded mountain range at the edge where they join, characterised by frequent earthquakes as the land masses fuse together. If on the other hand one of the colliding edges is an ocean crust, then the ocean crust, which is much denser, will glide under the continental mass. A rare exception to this is found in Oman, where a large block of deep ocean crust forms the hills behind Muscat. As the ocean crust sinks, it heats up under the influence of increasing pressure and rising ambient temperature. At depths greater than 100 kilometres this heating is so great that all or some of the descending plate's minerals melt and turn into liquid magma. Part of this magma forces its way violently to the surface through the weakest part of the overlying crust and creates a string of volcanoes on the surface parallel to the plate edge. The Asir island-arc was the product of such a collision between two small plates about one billion years ago.

The coast of Africa at that time did not extend beyond the line of the present-day River Nile. East of that line was the ocean, with the Asir island-arc

Above: *The earth's crust rides on the mantle. To a depth of 100 km the mantle is hard and rock-like, but below this depth it becomes increasingly plastic and fluid. Below 350 km it again becomes hard, because despite its increasing heat the overlying pressure keeps it rigid.*

EVOLUTION OF AN ISLAND-ARC

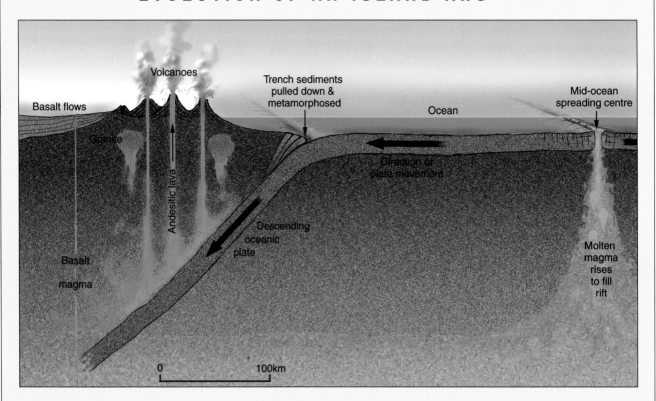

The descending plate of basalt ocean crust sinks towards the mantle, until it becomes hot enough for some of its minerals to melt. This molten mix is pushed upwards and erupts on the surface, building up volcanoes which eventually emerge from the sea. The rock they form is often andesite, which is a highly viscous magma which flows poorly. This high viscosity means that the volcanoes are high and steep-sided. The descending plate eventually reaches a depth where all its minerals melt, and large quantities of basalt erupt into the basin behind the volcanic line. Much of the rising magma does not reach the surface and forces out immense chambers in the crust, where it slowly cools. The crust above rises in consequence. Where the two plates grind together, large chunks at the edge of one plate break off and the rock, a mixture of basalt from the plate and ocean-floor sediments, is carried some way under the surface. There, it is heated and pressurised, not sufficiently to melt it but sufficiently to change its nature or 'metamorphose' it.

far offshore. The next 400 million years is a story of how the area of the sea offshore northeast Africa became land; how the tectonic processes produced Arabia, and incidentally eastern Egypt and Sudan

It involved a succession of plate collisions. The oldest were the three westernmost plates, successively pushing against each other until they formed a single unit. Two or perhaps three further small plates moving from the east then consecutively collided with that new consolidated plate, until the whole mass was securely united, both within itself and with the African continent.

The first land mass to appear, the Asir island-arc, had developed into a complex homogeneous block of land by the time a second collision started to create the Hejaz arc to the north a hundred million years later. By then the original volcanic chain, which ran partly where Bisha and Taif now stand, had been unroofed and worn down by erosion. The debris was carried down by rain to fill the basins before and behind the volcanic chain with broken rock, which in time was consolidated into sedimentary rock of various kinds. Since this activity long predated the first land vegetation, erosion would have been fierce. Layer upon layer of alternating rock types were formed, the deeper ones being crushed and altered by the pressure from overlying strata. As the volcanoes wore down, the rocks which had originally cooled deep within them were exposed as areas of granite, diorite and many others. The final result was a relatively flat landscape, with outcrops of old igneous rocks standing up through the newer sediments.

The same inevitable processes happened to each arc in turn. After the Hejaz arc collided with the Midian plate to the north, the series of small plates to the east Afif, Al Amar and Ar Rayn all went through similar stages of development.

Below: *How the colliding island-arcs of Hejaz and Azir may have looked about 750 million years ago. Volcanism in the Asir arc on the left has died down. The central portion (A) will shrink further as the plate descends. The Hejaz arc is growing, and will consolidate with the Asir arc. The four towns along the bottom show roughly where this land appears in today's Arabia.*

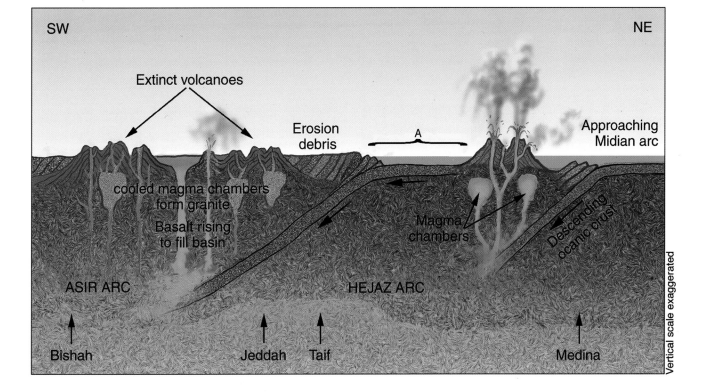

IGNEOUS ROCK

Igneous rock is rock which has cooled and solidified from a previously molten liquid state. 95% of the earth's crust is igneous, and starts life as a magma composed of different percentages of six principal minerals. The commonest rocks into which magmas solidify are shown in the chart below, together with the minerals of which they are composed. In each case, a magma of a given mineral composition may cool into one of two common rocks, depending on the rate at which it cools. The minerals in a slow-coolng magma have time to crystallise, so individual crystals will be larger and obvious to the naked eye. Conversely, a magma which cools rapidly gives the minerals in it little or no time to crystallise, so the appearance of the rock is fine and even-textured.

Basalt is a fast-cooled rock. It has a dark smooth surface, with no obvious crystals; it forms by being ejected rapidly onto the earth's surface through volcanoes, and is by far the commonest rock in the *harrats*, or lava fields, of the Hejaz.

By contrast, granite has a rough speckled texture with individual crystals clearly visible; it has always solidified slowly in very large masses deep underground.

Both these rocks are common in the Shield, much commoner than rhyolite or gabbro, the alternate forms which their magmas may take (see chart). This is because granitic magma is highly viscous and stops flowing when its temperature drops only slightly. It therefore seldom reaches the surface. Basaltic magma, on the other hand, flows easily, and rises fast through the crust, so is commonly extruded onto the earth's surface. Incidentally, granite

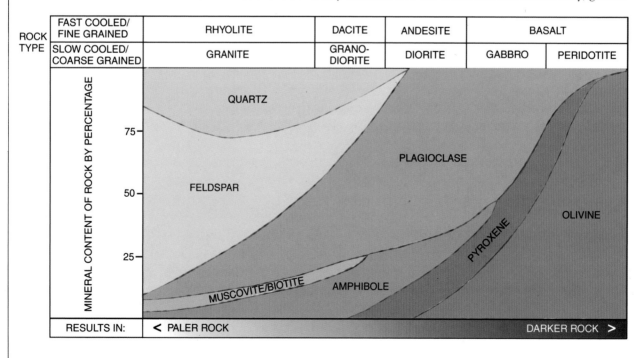

is only seen in the landscape because great thicknesses of rock have been eroded from the land which once covered it.

By careful study of the chart it will be possible to make an approximate identification of rock type for many igneous rock specimens. There are, however, many hundreds of less common igneous rocks, which it is beyond the scope of this book to describe.

Above: *The dark line of a dyke in central Najd, running sometimes for many kilometres across the surface of the Shield, reveals where upwelling magma has found a weakness in the surface rocks. These dykes can form walls across the landscape since they typically consist of harder rock, and are therefore more resistant to erosion than the surrounding host rock .*

Above: *The dark lines running across this hillside near Tabuk in the far north-wes t of Arabia are dykes. Pressure on underground magma masses has forced them upwards through weaknesses and faults in the overlying rock. Erosion now reveals where they cooled.*

Below: *The jagged outlines of the massif of Hissat ibn Huwail in central Arabia are typical of the granite hills of the Arabian Shield. 500 million years of erosion have removed the great thickness of rock which once lay over the granite and have carved the picturesque silhouettes into the granite massif.*

METAMORPHIC ROCK

Above: *Schist commonly cleaves into slabs and plates, and weathered schist surfaces such as these have a distinctive appearance which is readily recognisable from a distance. Note how the small schist hill near Ar Rayn in Najd has been folded so that the rock now lies at an angle of 90 degrees to the original bedding.*

Opposite: *One striking example of a metamorphic rock is this spindle schist. It fractures into long thin rods reminiscent of a spindle. This example is exposed in a road cutting south of Medina.*

The rocks of the Shield are not all igneous. Throughout the ages when the Arabian plate was being formed erosion was continually breaking down the new land into fragments to be consolidated as sedimentary rock of different kinds. These early sedimentary rocks were in turn caught up in the tectonic chaos, buried under new layers of sediment, lava and ash, or carried down by the descending plate. If buried deeply enough they would remelt; if not, they sometimes retained their original hard consistency but changed their mineral composition under the influences of increasing heat and pressure. Just as baking changes a set of individual ingredients into a cake, so heat can change rock. This process is called metamorphism. Common effects of metamorphism are:–

    a) a growth in the grain size of component minerals

    b) a tendency for the growing minerals to form parallel foliations or stripes, frequently highly folded

    c) a recombination of existing minerals to form distinctive new minerals

The degree and duration of the heating and pressure to which the original rock is subject, and the speed or slowness of the subsequent cooling, will determine the final rock produced. Common metamorphic rocks are:–

* slate, schist and gneiss (all derived from sedimentary shale but subject
  to different degrees of heating)
* marble, derived from limestone
* quartzite, derived from sandstone
* greenschist, the abundant result of basalt metamorphism

Deep burial is one way to produce the conditions required, but not the only one. For example, when magma thrusts through joints in overlying rock to produce dykes the intense heat of the magma will metamorphose the adjacent rock. The widespread emplacement of granite masses in the Shield resulted in each case in a narrow band of metamorphism in the surrounding rocks. This is known as contact metamorphism.

AGE	EVENT
1000	Early stages of Asir arc formation
800	Hejaz arc begins to emerge
	Mountain building in Asir
750	Asir & Hejaz arcs collide
700	
	Hejaz continues to build
650	Hejaz collides with Midyan Arc
	Collision of Afif and Ar Rayn
600	
	Arabian shield consolidated
	Granite emplacements under shield
550	Faulting mainly N.W.-S.E. orientated
	Stability of shield

(left margin, vertical: MILLION YEARS)

A simplified time chart showing the main events and their relative ages in the development of the Arabian Shield.

The result each time was a *mélange* of different rocks.

One particular rock series has helped geologists to piece together this sequence. As an ocean plate descends, small pieces of the descending ocean plate may break off and be left behind near the place where the two plates collided, to be exposed by later erosion. They are known as ophiolites, and are distinctive, since they have the same composition as oceanic crust: they contain basalt pillow lavas, which look like extruded toothpaste, and complex parallel sheets of basalt and gabbro (an igneous rock of the same mineral composition as basalt, but cooled more slowly and therefore having a more pronounced crystalline texture). Since this rock sequence only forms on ocean floors its presence on land is an excellent guide to where the edges, or sutures, of old plate boundaries lay.

The process of accretion into a single plate seems to have ended about 640 million years ago with the final addition of the Ar Rayn plate. The early history of the Ar Rayn plate is poorly understood by geologists but analysis of its rocks suggests that it

Above: *A granite outcrop at the Eastern edge of the Shield.*

Above right: *A smooth homogeneous face of granite towers behind the eroding ridge in the foreground. Weathering granite tends to produce rounded boulders with typical onion-skin layering.*

was already a block of ancient continental crust by the time it collided with the growing plate to the west. Although it was now a structural unit, the new plate was to see almost a hundred million more years of tectonic activity before it became quiet. Very large quantities of magma were emplaced beneath its surface, to cool slowly into granite masses; strains and stresses as it settled down caused the new land to crack and fault significantly; and large volumes of volcanic lava flowed onto the surface to mingle with the sedimentary rocks created from the eroded remnants of the first mountain chains. Around 550 million years ago this first phase of Arabia's formation ended. Thereafter there would be little tectonic disturbance of the new plate until the events leading to the opening of the Red Sea over 500 million years later.

This newly consolidated land mass is what we now call the Arabian Shield. Its rocks lie exposed in the western half of the peninsula; over much of central and all of eastern Arabia the Shield rocks cannot be seen because they are covered by later, younger rocks of sedimentary origin; the Shield rocks lie buried deep underneath.

Throughout the period of its formation, the Shield, this new land, had been crawling across the face of the globe. By 640 million years ago it lay well into the southern hemisphere: Jeddah would have lain at the same latitude then as Buenos Aires does today. The slow movements of the plates – a few centimetres a year – add up to remarkable global wandering. Arabia has for most of the last 600 million years been situated well south of the Equator. Some 300 million years ago it was further south than Patagonia and New Zealand are today. Scientists have pieced together this story using evidence from several different sources. Fossils, for example, show the types of vegetation and animal life existing at different past times. In Saudi Arabia

ARABIA'S COURSE ACROSS THE GLOBE

All the world's continents have been in continuous slow movement throughout geological history. Arabia's movement through different latitudes has been plotted by magnetic measurements and by the fossil record. Palaeozoic sediments are seen to have been deposited in cold or temperate climates; Triassic and later sediments demonstrate a fossil fauna typical of tropical climates.

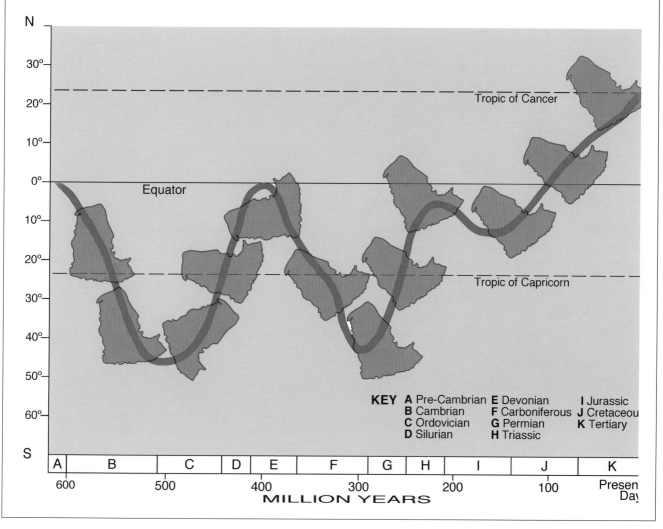

KEY A Pre-Cambrian E Devonian   I Jurassic
     B Cambrian   F Carboniferous J Cretaceou
     C Ordovician   G Permian   K Tertiary
     D Silurian   H Triassic

we find fossil evidence of glaciation, of tropical rain forest, in fact of most climatic environments. These could only have occurred if the peninsula had been elsewhere than its present position during those times. Another pointer is the magnetic orientation which rocks adopt when they form. Careful analysis of present magnetic orientation of rocks can demonstrate where on the globe they were when the rock was first laid down.

It was not only Afro-Arabia which was in motion; all the other plates were equally restless. For 400 million years after it came into being, Arabia was part of Gondwanaland, the super-continent consisting of Africa, South America, Australia, India and Madagascar. For a shorter time – between 300 and 200 million years ago – the northern continents also attached themselves to Gondwanaland, creating a single immense land mass of all the world's continents, which geologists know as Pangaea. Though the clues available to decipher these movements become fewer as we go back in time, it seems that an earlier Pangaea broke up and dispersed a little more than a billion years ago, that is to say just at the time when the Asir arc was first appearing.

GONDWANALAND

The great southern continent of 600-200 million years ago comprised the continents of today's southern hemisphere.

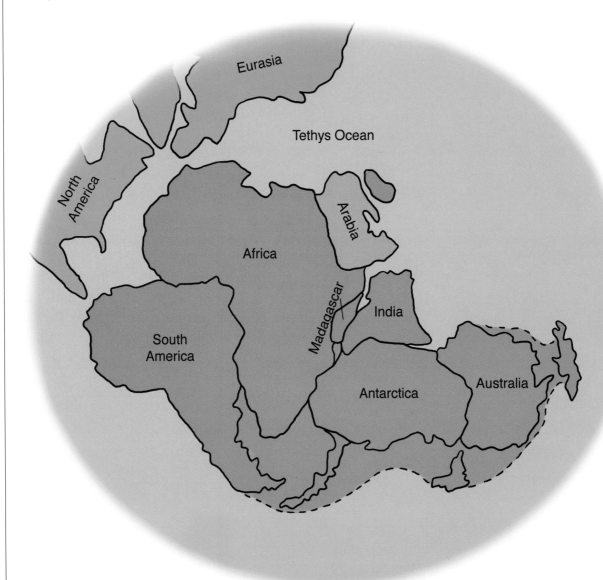

CHAPTER TWO

BUILDING ON THE SHIELD

The final completion of the Arabian Shield coincided with the start of a most remarkable period in the world's development. We followed the slow evolution of animal life earlier, and noted how few forms of life had evolved during the long ages before the Shield came into being. Then, about 600 million years ago, an immense diversity of animal forms suddenly began to blossom in the world's seas. In less than 100 million years the ancestral forms of all the great classes, or phyla, of living creatures now on earth had evolved. No new phyla have emerged since then. Amazingly, all those original phyla are represented today. While almost all species of all those phyla have died out, a few species survived to continue the line of descent of the unique characteristics of each phylum. No other period before or since has seen such evolutionary creativity.

Arabia at the time was a vast barren plain with few prominent features on it: the earlier hills and mountains had largely been eroded away. In imagining how the land looked then we must bear in mind that landscape features we see

Below: *The oldest sedimentary rocks in the Arabian peninsula lie in northwest Arabia. In the area around Tabuk ancient Cambrian sandstone was laid down on the worn grey rocks of the Shield. The red sandstone cliff in the photograph is about 500 million years old.*

Above, left: *The Cambrian sandstone weathers into fantastic spires and towers, as here in Wadi Qaraqir south of Tabuk. The rock, though well exposed, is almost devoid of fossils, as complex life as we know it was only just coming into being at the time these rocks were formed. Today the porous sandstone acts as an aquifer from which small perennial streams flow for a short distance before being swallowed by the sandy wadi floors.*

today – the western mountains, the Red Sea, the central escarpments – are all much younger. Onto this eroded surface now crept the sea, animated by its new and diverse animal life. Starting about 550 million years ago world sea levels rose continuously for seventy million years. As they did so, the sea encroached more and more over Arabia, until the only parts remaining as dry land were the northwest, the region around Tabuk and perhaps some ground in the southwest in Yemen.

By 470 million years ago the shallow seas were ebbing away, leaving behind on the surface of the Shield a layer several hundreds of metres thick of mixed sand and mud sediments. Very few features of the original Shield stood proud of this new surface.

Many of those sediments were eroded away by subsequent events, for soon after the peninsula emerged as dry land its western half was covered in thick ice sheets. The global drift of the continent had taken Arabia to the most southerly position it was to reach; western Arabia was at a latitude south of Tierra del Fuego's present position, and Africa stretched south to cover the south pole. The glacier fields which covered central Africa now reached out to blanket most of Arabia. In Qassim are ancient sedimentary rocks known as till, of a type peculiar to glacier fields, which tell the story. The glaciers ground away the land which they covered, reworking the sediments into rock flour, boulder fields and other typical glacial remains. When the ice melted the land it had occupied looked very different. The previously flat landscape was riven with valleys cut by the glaciers, with jumbled piles of boulders and gravel choking their floors. To the east, between the glaciers and the sea, the sediment was eroded away by rivers draining melt water from the glaciers into the Tethys Sea. In the far southeast of the peninsular the oldest sediments in the Jebel Akhdar of Oman contain glacial features such as tills and striated boulders that also testify to this early glaciation.

Time eventually carried Arabia and the rest of Gondwanaland away

Left: *Glaciers such as this covered much of Arabia in the Carboniferous period. The great weight of the ice sheet scored grooves in the rocks over which it moved, leaving behind a record of is progress.*

SEDIMENTARY ROCK

As soon as a rock is formed on the surface of the land, nature's various agencies set to work to destroy it. Wind and frost, rain and ice all combine to wear it away, shattering the surface into boulders, breaking the boulders into cobbles and pebbles, and working individual mineral grains out of the pebbles to make sand silt and clay. The broken particles, carried downhill by rivers and by gravity, may eventually remain static for a long time or they may be covered by a further layer of detritus, in which case they will be compressed firmly together. Circulating groundwater will film them with calcite or some similar mineral which will cement them together until they form a solid whole. This will be a sedimentary rock. All sedimentary rock, of which there are many kinds, are essentially rocks composed of individual particles assembled together and cemented into a new coherent rock.

Sediments created on land are classified according to the size of particles which make them up. The main categories are:–

NAME	CONSISTENCY
Conglomerate	Made of pebbles or larger stones, commonly rounded.
Breccia	As conglomerate, but stones tend to be angular.
Sandstone	Made of cemented sand grains; grain size varies up to 2mm. but grains can be seen with simple magnifying glass. Quartz is by far the principal sand mineral.
Shale	Very fine-grained sediment made of clay and silt. Often splits or flakes horizontally. Sometimes called siltstone or mudstone.

Most nonmarine sedimentary rocks of these types in Arabia are made of material eroded off the original Shield hills and mountains in pre-Cambrian times.

One of the most common rocks in Arabia is limestone. This also is sedimentary, though formed underwater. It consists of calcium minerals which

Below: *An example of conglomerate*

Below right: *An example of breccia*

Above: *An example of sandstone: the remarkable facades and chambers at Medain Saleh are all carved out of some of the earliest sedimentary rock in Arabia.*

reach the sea-floor in one of two ways. Either they are precipitated chemically directly out of sea water in certain marine environments to build up on the sea floor as a smooth fine homogeneous rock, usually white in colour; or they are absorbed by corals, sea urchins, molluscs and other creatures to form shells and skeletons which fall to the sea bed when the animal dies. Frequently we find limestone which combines both origins.

The third principal type of sedimentary rock is evaporites. These form in shallow warm enclosed bodies of water – lakes, inland seas and *sabkhas* – when the water evaporates faster than it is replaced. When these conditions occur, the result is progressively more saline water, until the salts precipitate to the bottom. Depending on which salts are dissolved in the water the rock which forms will be halite, anhydrite, gypsum or common salt. Exposed to weathering, evaporites erode and dissolve quickly, and so are rarely seen exposed in surface outcrops.

We have sketched in the principal rock categories, but there are many gradations between these types, and many intermediate or unusual mixes of materials which give rise to rarer or more localised types of sedimentary rock. To take one example, there are large beds of phosphorite near the Jordan border in the north, which are a promising source of industrial phosphate. These phosphorite deposits are an Eocene marine sediment formed of phosphorus-rich organic matter, plankton debris, diatom skeletons, fish bones and teeth, all mixed with calcite. The high phosphorus content of the sediment material, and the particular bacterial action on it when deposited, has turned it into phosphorite.

FOSSILS

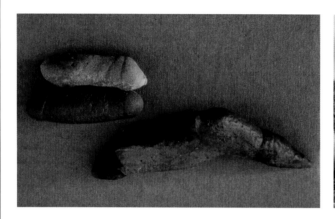

Above: *Fossil dung from an Eocene crocodile. Even when no trace remains of the animal itself, coprolites such as these, or footprints solidified in the mud, can show that it lived here at a certain time.*

Above: *A specimen of fossil petrified wood shows, on the right, how features of the bark and original form of the wood can be preserved. On the left, a slice through the hard calcite of a fossil log retains traces of the original structure of the wood.*

When an animal or plant dies its remains are normally consumed by bacterial or chemical action and recycled into the chain of life, leaving no trace behind. Fossils are the rare exceptions to this: physical traces of a creature preserved in sedimentary rock. The fossil imprint is very seldom of the same mineral composition as the original. The bone, flesh, bark, wood and shell of the living creature all decay, but slowly enough for the sediment into which they fell to have hardened before their disintegration. Soft-bodied creatures such as jellyfish are very rarely preserved, for obvious reasons; animals with a hard bony skeleton or shell are more commonly preserved because the slow rate of decay of their skeletons allows sediment to build up and harden around them before they vanish. As the original forms dissolve, their place is taken by a mineral deposit carried in by circulating groundwater, which fills the now consolidated mould and preserves the shape of the creature. Sometimes the evidence for an animal's existence is even more tenuous: fossil dung, known as coprolites, are common, as are worm casts or burrows made by worms and other soft-bodied animals. The animals themselves may not be found but their existence can be inferred.

Fossils are our only source of knowledge of the living world of past ages. For more than a century palaeontologists have been fitting newly discovered fossil specimens into place in the history of evolution, noting how phyla split into genera, and genera into species, and how each species has altered its form over the ages in order to adapt to changing environments.

Index Fossils

In dating a fossil-bearing rock, scientists will compare the particular fossils found within it with data from previous discoveries of the same fossils elsewhere. Many types of animal were widely distributed around the world, and a fossil fauna from one location can be confidently correlated in time with a similar fauna found elsewhere. Species in general do not have very long life spans, though there are some spectacular exceptions to this general rule. Coelecanth fish, lungfish and horseshoe crabs are well-known examples of very long and unchanging lineages; they survive today almost unchanged from their ancestors found in Devonian rocks of 400 million years ago. The average mammal species appears to have survived on average for about five million years before becoming extinct, yielding its place to a successor species.

The most useful species for the geologist trying to date the rocks he is studying are those that had a wide geographical spread as well as a short species life span. Graptolites and ammonites, for example, fit these criteria well: they appear to have undergone frequent modification, with new species frequently arising to replace for a relatively brief period their predecessor species. Data from ammonite studies elsewhere

Above, above left: Although most fossils are traces of living forms, here what has been preserved is an ancient Jurassic beach, with the ripples in the sand frozen in time, conforming to the same pattern as wind- or water-blown sand today.

Top left: Part of a large ammonite from the Jurassic escarpment of the Jebel Tuwaiq.

Top right: Sea urchins are part of the extensive echinoderm (literally: spiny-skin) phylum. Here a group of different species of urchins shows how they vary widely in size, but are frequently well preserved in the fossil record. One branch of this phylum consists of creatures called crinoids or sea-lilies (though they are animals, not plants), which anchor themselves to the sea-bed by a long stalk or stem. Fragments of the stem are frequently preserved as fossils, such as the three Jurassic specimens on the lower left of the photograph.

helped to date the sequence of Jurassic rocks in the Jabal Tuwaiq escarpment, where many ammonite species are found.

The search for oil and water is made by drilling deep holes through sedimentary rock. To control the process drillers will want to explore a particular stratum, perhaps because it has shown promise in another well, or in an outcrop of rock some distance away. To know they have found the same stratum they must usually find the same fossils as were present in the other well or outcrop. The diameters of their drill holes, and therefore the size of the rock samples they can draw up for examination, are small, so useful fossils from their point of view are those which are extremely abundant and extremely small. Pollen grains and spores from ancient plants are very suitable; minute, but when viewed under a microscope are each seen to have a recognisably distinct form. So too with foraminifera and radiolarians, two very diverse and ancient groups of amoeba-like animals. They range in diminutive size from 0.05mm. to 1mm, but despite being so small their shells show a diversity and intricacy at least the equal of any seashells seen on the world's beaches. Appearing first in Ordovician times, they continue to be widespread in today's oceans. As their many species have evolved and shell patterns changed, they have left an excellent index for determining the age of marine sedimentary rock.

from the polar region and into warmer latitudes. The glaciers retreated and the
sea once again covered most of the peninsula except for the northwest; this
second marine invasion also left behind a thick sediment,this time a shale
containing many fossil graptolites. These now extinct animals were one of the
most numerous inhabitants of the seas between 550 and 350 million years ago;
they belonged to the same phylum as modern hydras, jellyfish, corals and sea-
anemones. Like jellyfish, they were free swimming; but like corals they consisted
of a colony of polyps. Graptolites quickly branched into numerous different
species, most with a rather short span of existence, so they are useful index
fossils. This graptolite shale, rich in organic matter, is the source of several vast
hydrocarbon resources. In Qatar the immense gas reserves of the North Dome
field formed out of the organic content of this 420 million year old sediment.

   For the second time in its history Arabia emerged from the sea, layered with

Three of the numerous species of graptolite.

its new coating of shale. The difference this time was that, as it emerged, the
margins of its lakes, rivers and coastline were tinged with green. Plant life in
this Silurian age first adapted to life ashore, to be followed quite soon by animal
life. By now the ozone layer, a by-product of the oxygen-rich air, had thickened
in the upper atmosphere, providing a shield against the intense solar ultra-
violet rays. Without it, life on land could hardly have come into being in
anything like its present form.

   For both arthropods and amphibians (the first two animal groups to colonise
the land) there must have been a long period of adaptation as they developed
breathing apparatus suitable for absorbing oxygen from the air rather than the
water. Life must have hovered around the water's edge until lungs and legs had
adapted to the new environment. Arabia was then astride the tropic of
Capricorn and provided a warm sub-tropical scene for these tentative first steps
on land.

   A dozen more times in its history Arabia was to be covered by the sea, and
as often to emerge. Indeed it has been under water twice as long as it has been
above sea level. The first of these successive inundations was in the Devonian
period, about 400 million years ago. Rare fossils of this period have been found

GEOLOGICAL TIME SCALE

Millions of years before Present	Eras	Periods	Epochs	Duration of Eras (millions of years)
.01	CENOZOIC	Quaternary	Recent	65
1.6			Pleistocene	
5		Tertiary	Pliocene	
23			Miocene	
35			Oligocene	
56			Eocene	
65			Paleocene	
145	MESOZOIC	Cretaceous	E	180
208		Jurassic	E	
245		Triassic	E	
290	PALEOZOIC	Permian	E	325
360		Carboniferous		
408		Devonian	E	
438		Silurian		
510		Ordovician	E	
570		Cambrian	E	

KEY: E = Extinction Event

The development of larger, more complex life forms in the period after 570 million years ago began to increase the frequency of fossil forms preserved in rocks after that time. There is a commonly used geological time-scale for rocks, reproduced above. The divisions on the time-scale are determined by the fossil record. Each period is defined by a particular type of fossil fauna and flora. Species are constantly evolving, with new ones appearing and existing species disappearing from the record. Occasionally there is a wholesale change, when a high percentage of all species suddenly disappears, its ecological place taken by newly evolved species. Nine or ten times since the start of the Cambrian which itself designates the first flowering of complex multi-cellular life forms there have occurred wholesale changes in the fossil record sufficiently dramatic for the new animal and plant assemblage to be known by a new name. These names are in a sense a short-hand way of describing a certain broad category of flora and fauna, though they are used to denote a period of geological time.

It is widely known that dinosaurs died off within a geologically short period of time, with their ecological niche being then occupied by mammals (marsupial mammals in Australasia and South America, placental mammals elsewhere). This occurred about 65 million years ago. But the dinosaurs were not alone. Over 60% of all the world's species of living creatures failed to survive that time. To describe this change, geologists say the Cretaceous period ended then and the Palaeocene epoch began. Though, thanks to the glamour of dinosaurs, this end-Cretaceous extinction event is the most famous of its kind, it was not the most severely threatening to the continuation of life on earth. 245 million years ago a catastrophe of unknown cause struck the world. Perhaps the cause was the explosive impact of a comet or giant meteor with the earth, throwing all habitats and ecosystems into disarray. Global cooling caused by clouds of dust thrown up by a series of impacts by meteors or comets are considered to be a probable contributory factor. Whatever the cause, only 5-15% of the species recorded in rocks of the Permian period survived into the Triassic period. That event seems to have been the closest shave the animal kingdom has had with total extinction. Triassic fossils are almost all new species, descendants of the few survivors from Permian times, now multiplying and diversifying easily in an empty world to fill the niches formerly occupied by the extinct Permian fauna.

Left: *The Jibal Wajid are a large Permian sandstone massif north of Najran. Highly eroded, they break up on their eastern edge into isolated rock hills, as here, before disappearing beneath the sands of the Empty Quarter.*

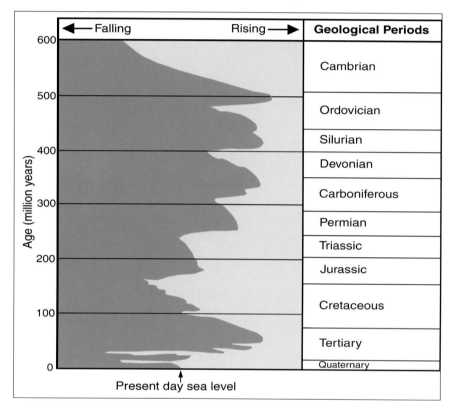

Left: *Global sea levels have fluctuated quite widely since the emplacement of the Arabian Shield. The chart shows the relative changes over time. Several factors appear to play a part in these changes, of which the two most important are glaciation and plate tectonics.*

Glaciation can lock up very large quantities of water. As polar ice-sheets thicken at the height of a glaciation, sea levels drop; as global climate warms and the ice-sheets shrink so the sea levels rise.

Plate tectonics can influence sea levels by reducing the total area of continental crust by mountain-building during continued collisions, which would reduce sea levels. Sea floor rises and the height of mid-ocean ridges may also fluctuate thus reducing or expanding the volume of the ocean basins, which in turn should also affect sea levels.

both near Najran in the south and Al Jawf in the north, in the form of Devonian fish scales, spines and bones.

For reasons that are not well understood, land masses can rise and fall, independent of sea levels or tectonic activity, but probably connected with some deep-seated action in the mantle. There may be no deformation in the plate, no mountain-building; the land gently rises as a block. Arabia has risen and fallen in this way several times.

About 375 million years ago one of these episodes occurred; Arabia emerged from the sea as dry land, at a time when sea levels were static. One of the most interesting geological feature to have survived from the succeeding period is a number of granite boulder beds in early Permian sediments at the southernmost tip of the Jebel Tuwaiq, where it disappears into the sands of the Rub Al Khali. These boulders vary in size up to five feet across and yet they are a hundred

Opposite: *The Jurassic age in Arabia was a time when the land was covered by warm tropical seas. On the sea bed were deposited great thicknesses of limestone, sometimes highly fossiliferous, which are now exposed in the Tuwaiq escarpment, as here near Riyadh.*

Above: *The cast of a Jurassic gastropod. Very often the shell of a fossil has been dissolved, leaving only an impression or mould of the inside of the animal's shell. The impression is limestone, like the surrounding rock.*

Above: *A number of marine fossils from the upper Jurassic strata of the Tuwaiq, including gastropods, bivalves and brachiopods. The small cup-like objects in the centre are the skeletons of porifera sponges.*

Above: *Many different kinds of corals can be found in the Tuwaiq. Here the tip of a large reef-forming coral protrudes from the surrounding limestone.*

Above: *Around Hawtah, south of Riyadh, the Tuwaiq escarpment is broken by numerous wadis such as this, edged with Jurassic limestone cliffs. Before being washed onto the thick gravel floor of the wadi, the debris from the eroding cliffs forms a sloping scree or talus slope such as the one on the right of the photograph. These slopes frequently contain Jurassic fossils which have broken away from their surrounding rock.*

Left: *The uniformity of the Tuwaiq escarpment edge is broken occasionally by wadis and by outlying hills and mesas. This spectacular landmark is one of several in the Wadi Nissah system.*

Above left: *As the Tuwaiq escarpment marches south the uniform limestone thicknesses in the Riyadh area change to a more mixed sequence of rock types. Jebel Baloum, in the photograph, is an outlier from the main escarpment west of Hawtah. Sandstone at its lower levels mixed with conglomerate and shale, give way towards the summit to a white limestone.*

EROSION

Erosion is the process by which rock is broken down and transported to lower levels. Water is far and away the principal agent in this movement, in the form of rain, streams and rivers. Other agents such as wind, ice and frost also play a part, and sometimes a locally or visually distinctive one, but in fact very minor overall.

The process is continual but proceeds at different rates. In today's Arabia, with its low rainfall, erosion is very slow. There are no rivers to carry the rock away. Occasional flash floods have a temporary local effect, sandstorms move the lightest dust and silt across the surface, and wind rearranges the crests of the dunes; but little happens to change the landscape more widely.

At many times in the past Arabia has seen much greater rainfall. The sand and gravel which now covers eastern Arabia was transported there from the Shield by river. The truncated escarpment faces in central Arabia were pushed back by heavy water erosion. Further back in time the Shield itself was eroded flat. The fact that it is now in jagged relief is because the west of the country was uplifted quite recently and exposed once more to erosion, which will continue until the mountains are again reduced to a flat plain. The history of erosion is recorded in the rocks. If two sedimentary strata do not lie continuously parallel to each other it is because the lower level has been eroded. This irregular join is known as an *unconformity*.

Types of *unconformity*:–

Above: *Sediment is laid down in horizontal strata. But when the sand or silt is pushed by powerful currents of water or air – in fast flowing rivers or sand dunes – the bedding plane within the stratum is inclined at an angle from the horizontal. Here, in an early Jurassic sandstone on Jebel Baloum, the sloping central stratum reveals a time when a fast flowing river ran through the area.*

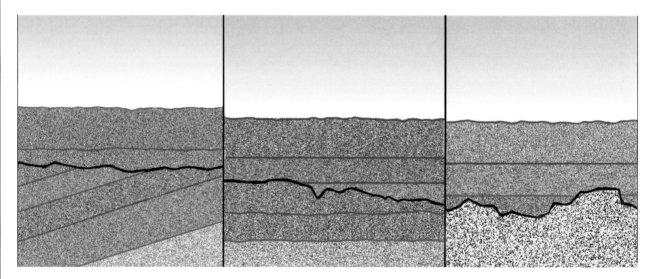

Angular Unconformity *shows lower (older) sediments deformed and eroded before younger rocks were formed..*

A Disconformity *appears when the join in two parallel strata shows erosion features in the lower rock.*

A Nonconformity *shows the (unconformable) join between igneous or metamorphic rock and stratified rocks above.*

Looking at the sedimentary record of Arabia, we find many *unconformities*, each of which records a phase of erosion. Note that diferent regions of the peninsula could be and were subject to different climatic regimes at the same time. During the Jurassic period, for example, while the east and centre were being built up by shallow water limestone deposition the Shield area to the west was being eroded by tropical rainstorms. A good example of a *nonconformity* can be seen at Quwayiyah on the Riyadh-Jeddah highway; there Permian limestone is laid directly on to Shield

Above: *The rough contours of the dark rocks of the Shield contrast with the pale horizontal strata of limestone above. The limestone dates from Permian times; all traces of earlier Palaeozoic sediments have been eroded away, and the Shield rocks themselves have suffered erosion before the limestone was deposited. The join between these two distinctly different rock types is known as a* nonconformity.

Above: *Although most escarpment and wadi edges have been worn back by erosion, a few such as Shaib Awsat and Wadi Nissah are the product of faults, which have caused the land bounded by the wadi sides to sink. The photograph shows Wadi Nissah. Compare with the diagram on pagexx.*

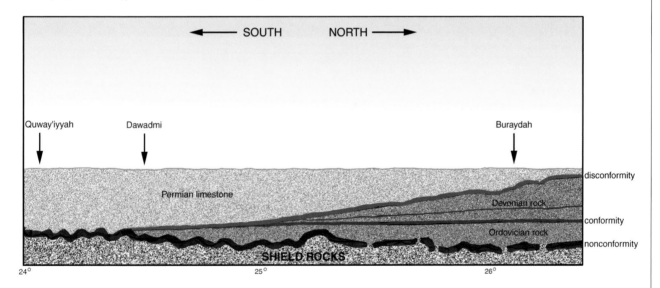

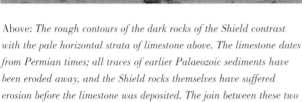

The vertical section is much exaggerated. The diagram shows a cross-section underlying the Permian Khuff formation in Nejd. It illustrated two unconformities common in Saudi Arabia. Because there has been so little deformation and folding of sedimentary rocks thanks to the Shield's long-term stability, examples of angular unconformities are rare.

rocks; all traces of the rocks formed between the creation of the Shield and Permian times, 300 million years, were eroded away before the limestone formed. Further north, near Unayzah in Qassim, the same limestone stratum rests on eroded Devonian and Ordovician rocks (a *disconformity*) showing that erosion in that area had been less severe, insufficient to destroy the earlier sedimentary rocks entirely.

FAULTS

Compression or tension of the earth's crust can cause the rock to split and deform along fault lines. The Red Sea valley is a tensional fault. In Nejd, a long tensional fault runs south from Majma'ah before swinging east to form Wadi Nissah and Wadi Sahba, probably the result of different stresses to the north and south during late Mesozoic times.

Tension causes a trench-like structure known as a graben when parallel fault lines move apart. A half-graben is a trench formed when a curved fault surface develops.

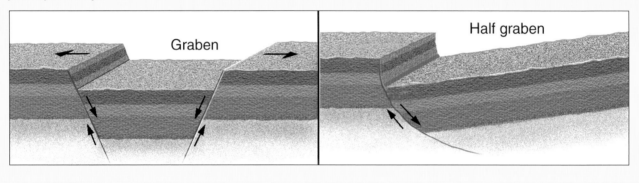

kilometres from the nearest granite outcrop from which they might have originated, which is in Yemen. For long a puzzle, they are now recognised as having been transported there by glacial action, at the same time as glaciers are known to have scoured Oman in the late Carboniferous or early Permian times. Arabia's course had again, and for the last time, taken it south to very low latitudes, and Antarctic glaciers covered the south of the land. The boulders may have been pushed north by the advancing ice-fields, though they do not show the grooves and striations usually present on rocks that have been moved in this way, or they may be dropstones. Dropstones are boulders, picked up and frozen into ice-floes, which drop out as the floe melts downstream. No other agency than glaciation could have moved such large boulders over the distance. In Oman, vivid geological testimony to this glacial phase can be seen in the bed of Wadi Al Khlata, where flat beds of rock are scored by parallel grooves up to a metre deep, gouged out by boulders embedded in a moving glacier. Thick sandstone sequences were built up during Permian times, and although now much eaten away by erosion still show up picturesquely in the Jibal Wajid, in southwest Arabia. They contain almost no large fossils but have been dated by spores found in rock samples from the stratum and analysed microscopically.

The end of the Permian, the time of the greatest extinction of plant and animal life, came as the peninsula was once more emerging from the sea, this time draped in a blanket of white limestone. When it did so, the living world had greatly changed.

The Permian extinction marked the end of the Palaeozoic era. So many species were eliminated then that when the world's ecosystems recovered they were inhabited by very different populations. The trilobites which had dominated life in the seas until then were reduced to a few relict species. The new era, the Mesozoic, was the time of the reptiles, and in particular the dinosaurs. Birds, which first flew in the Mesozoic, are an adaptation of one of the dinosaur families.

Right: *Water percolating down into limestone frequently eats out underground streams and caverns. When the water emerges from the rock, calcium carbonate or travertine is gradually precipitated from the water. Here a seep of water flowing out of the limestone cliff at Hawtah has built up a great mass of such rock in the lower half of the photograph. It can be recognised by the absence of horizontal strata and its slightly darker coloration.*

LANDFORMS

Sedimentary rocks erode to form different landscapes depending on their dip away from horizontal. A steep dip – uncommon in Saudi Arabia – gives rise to jagged relief; a low dip, typical of the sedimentary strata in Central Arabia, results in an escarpment forming at the higher end of the stratum. Flat dips produce mesas and irregular tablelands, which are also a feature of parts of Central Region.

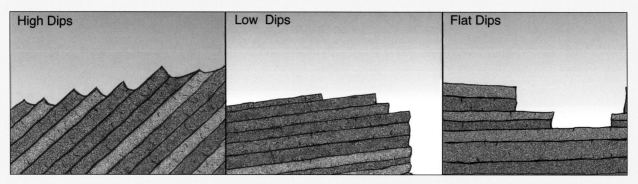

High Dips

Low Dips

Flat Dips

High Dips form a jagged terrain.

Low Dips result in escarpments, the top being a hard stratum resistant to weathering.

Flat Dips give rise to a tableland relief.

It was also the time when mammals evolved; they lived throughout the Mesozoic, as small and furtive creatures unable to challenge the dinosaurs' preeminence. Plant life changed remarkably, too. Lepidodendrons and giant horsetails gave way to cycads (tree ferns), conifers and, later, the true flowering plants which dominate today's vegetation.

These developments in the living world were helped by the break-up of Gondwanaland. The great southern continent broke apart soon after the start of the Mesozoic; Africa, India, Australia, South America and Antarctica all separated and spread out across the globe, multiplying enormously the range of favourable habitats for life. The sea shores of the new continents were several times as long as the old shore of Gondwana had been; and shallow coastal waters are one of the richest habitats. The continents enjoyed a more favourable climates as they moved out of the Antarctic belt, and their interiors were closer to the coast and rain-bearing weather. The very fact of their separation meant that wholly distinct flora and fauna could and did develop on each continent, adding to the diversity of life.

Arabia was now drifting continuously northwards into the tropics, crossing the Equator at about the end of the Jurassic age. Throughout Mesozoic times world sea levels rose, and by the end of the Cretaceous would stand at their highest levels since the Cambrian 400 million years before.

For much of this age Arabia was covered by shallow tropical seas. At first in thin limestone strata sandwiched between sandstone and shale layers, the Triassic and Jurassic rocks later built very considerable thicknesses of limestone. These can be seen today to be highly fossiliferous, with many reef features visible in well-exposed outcrops in the Jebel Tuwaiq escarpment. Corals are abundant, as are echinoids and molluscs. Ammonites, which were to die out at the same time as the dinosaurs at the end of the Cretaceous period, are also common.

How far west did these sea invasions penetrate? Did they cover the whole of Arabia and, if not, where did the furthest shoreline end? There are no precise answers to these questions. The western edges of the various strata give us a minimum distance, but it is also clear that these edges have in most cases been heavily eroded. The farthest shore then certainly lay west of today's strata.

In general it seems that the earlier invasions penetrated most deeply. A glance at the map shows the Cambrian and other early Palaeozoic sediments very close to the Red Sea both in the north and south. There is no trace of them on the Shield in the centre but we can safely attribute this to the effect of many periods of subsequent erosion.

Sediments from the end of the Palaeozoic and the Mesozoic, so well arrayed along an arc 1,000 kilometres long in the centre of the peninsula, probably reached as far west as a line joining the northern and southern tips of the outcrops, taking them to the vicinity of Afif on the Riyadh-Makkah road, 200 kilometres west of the closest Mesozoic marine sediment today.

East of the Tuwaiq escarpment the land continues its gradual dip to the east, and where the rock is exposed is seen to be almost exclusively limestone as far as the Dahna sand belt, with occasional beds of sandstone thinly layered into the marine sediments. This sequence of limestone represents ten different formations laid down on top of each other during the Jurassic and Cretaceous periods; the subsequent tilt of the land to the east combined with the effects of erosion allows each formation to be seen on the surface for a short distance before it is covered by the next more recent formation.

One striking exception to the limestone is to be seen at Dahl Hit, on the way to Al Kharj from Riyadh. Here is the only surface occurrence of an evaporite rock called anhydrite. The pearly gray rock shows very slight dark stains, which were recognised by Aramco geologists in 1938 as tar seeps, the first show of oil in Saudi Arabia and an important clue in deciphering the oil-bearing structures underlying the east of the country. When they then drilled down through this formation in the eastern Province they first tapped the country's immense oil reservoirs. Much of Arabia's oil lies in Jurassic formations, the limestones which crop out between the Tuwaiq escarpment and Riyadh, slightly older than the anhydrite. As these strata have become more deeply buried to the east, the rising pressure and temperatures have gently cooked them, releasing the oil. This has then been trapped under the anticlines folded into the rock as it was compressed by the later collision with Asia. The oil fields of southern Iraq and southern Iran lie under similar folds of the same age. The collision of Arabia with Asia which induced the folding is thus responsible for the preservation of close to half the world's oil reserves.

Towards the end of the Mesozoic the whole of central Arabia rose, as it had in the Devonian. The coastline was forced to retreat before the swelling land, shifting eastwards. It has never since moved inland very far; it has risen and fallen, and in successive pulses drowned the Eastern Province of Saudi Arabia and the other shore-lines of the Gulf several times, changing its physical nature dramatically as it did so; but it has not penetrated further west than a line where the Dahna sands run today. Henceforward central and western Arabia were to be a region of erosion and denudation, of terrestrial sediments built up by the reworking of older rock.

Above: *A slab of anhydrite from Dahl Hit. This evaporite rock is easily eroded and dissolved and is consequently little seen on the surface. In Dahl Hit the anhydrite stratum is protected from weathering by a cap of resistant limestone and can be well seen by those venturing down the slope to the interior of the dahl. The spot was well known in the past as a watering-hole for passers-by.*

CROSS-SECTION STRATA

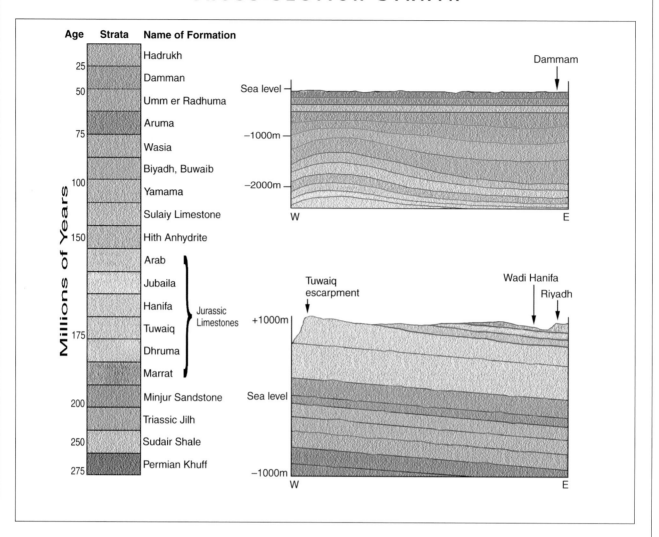

Cross-sections of sedimentary strata at two locations: above, under Riyadh and, below, under Dammam in Eastern Province. The vertical scale is exaggerated, but shows the dip of the strata from west to east. The pillar diagram shows the name and approximate age of each formation.

CHAPTER THREE

COLLISION WITH ASIA

THE ARABIAN PLATE

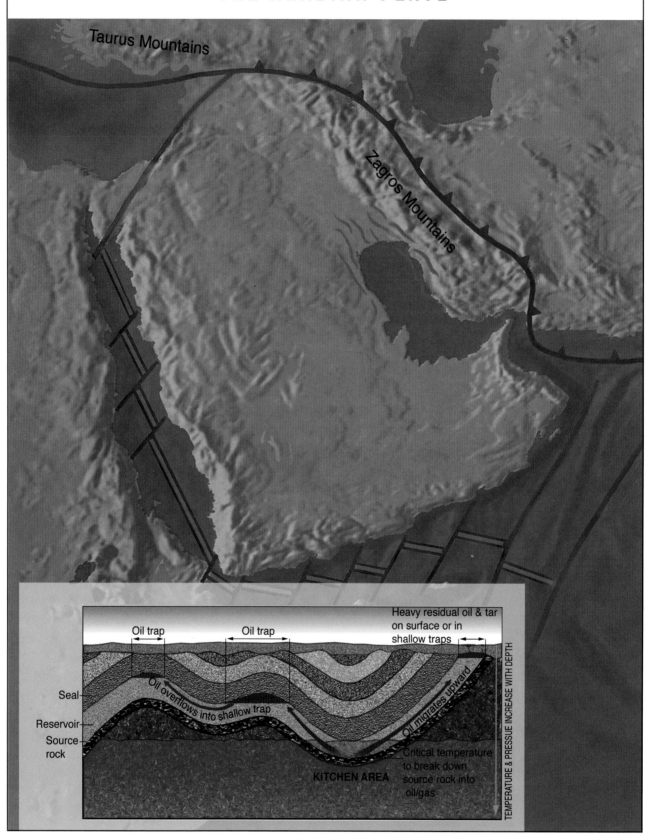

Taurus Mountains

Zagros Mountains

Oil trap

Oil trap

Heavy residual oil & tar on surface or in shallow traps

Seal

Oil overflows into shallow trap

Reservoir

Source rock

Oil migrates upward

Critical temperature to break down source rock into oil/gas

KITCHEN AREA

TEMPERATURE & PRESSURE INCREASE WITH DEPTH

Opposite: *The Arabian plate. The Taurus and
Zagros mountains rise where compression forces
have pushed the Arabian and Asian plates
together. The wavy blue parallel marks
delineate the gentle folds of the sedimentary
strata beneath which half of the world's oil is
trapped..*
Inset: *A cross-section of strata in the oil-bearing
region of the Gulf*

Next page, four scenes of Oman:
Clockwise from top left: *Isolated white
limestone boulders, sometimes very large, are
broken-off remnants of shallow submarine cliffs,
carried onto the Oman mainland on the darker
reddish deep-sea sediments 70 million years
ago.*

*A canyon eroded into the flanks of Jebel Shams,
the highest mountain in the Jebel Akhdar
range. The spectacular cliffs of layered
limestone plunge almost 1000 metres from the
high plateau to the green ribbon of the wadi far
below.*

*Evening light accentuates the contrast between
the dark pelagic sediments in the foreground
and the pale folded limestone mountain behind,
in the western Hajar mountains near Dariz.*

*One of the gorges which cuts into the central
bowl of the Jebel Akhdar. The strata both in the
foreground and at the rear can be seen to tilt at
a steep angle from the horizontal, the result of
the uplift and folding of the rock.*

We think of Arabia as part of Asia. The map shows it to be joined in the north and north-east to the rest of the Asian continent, while it is separated from Africa by the Red Sea. From the standpoint of geological history this is misleading.

As we have seen, Arabia was from its origin more than 500 million years ago an integral part of northeast Africa; the Arabian Shield and Nubian Shield were formed as one entity by the same forces at the same time, and did not separate until less than 50 million years ago, while the wide Tethys Sea had lain between Asia and Arabia since the time of Gondwanaland. As the Afro-Arabian plate drifted northeast towards Asia the Tethys gradually narrowed to a gulf when the shelves of the two continents first began to make contact about 50 million years ago, and closed completely as they ground more closely together.

The forces deep beneath the continents which propel the plates on their course across the globe are extremely powerful. Two continental masses in collision will continue to move towards each other until they are very firmly welded together. This process of compression results in a high folded mountain chain along the line where the continents meet. India's collision with Asia has created the Himalayas; in Europe, the Alps have been raised as Africa pushes Italy against Europe; the Urals are the more ancient result of the collision between Europe and Asia. In the Arabian peninsula the most striking folded mountains are the Jebel Akhdar in Oman. The tops of the Jebel Akhdar are made of marine limestone, and it is easy to collect old fossil seashells from the high crests of the mountains, pushed 2000 metres up from the old sea shore by collision and folding.

In the same way, the Arabian-Asian collision has forced up mountains along the north and northeast edges of the Arabian plate. The Zagros mountains in Iran and the Taurus mountains in southeast Turkey are the result. The Zagros are in part the crumpled remains of the same sedimentary formations which cover central and eastern Arabia, and which also extend under the Arabian Gulf and into what is now southern Iran. The easternmost edges of these formations have been folded and thrust up thousands of metres above sea level. There appear to have been numerous mountain-building episodes in the Zagros over the last 50 million years; even today the earthquakes common in the Zagros are evidence that the mountains are not yet wholly stable.

We saw earlier how tectonic plates behave when they collide, with denser oceanic crust sinking beneath continental crust. There are rare instances of the opposite happening, with oceanic crust overriding a continent. One of the world's most extensive and best-preserved examples of this is the Hajar mountains of Northern Oman. In late Cretaceous times, when the Arabian and Asian plates were beginning to make contact, a belt of oceanic crust pushed onto the shallow-water limestone of coastal Arabia to cover what is now northern Oman.

As the collision between the two plates progressed, the compression forced this new land up, folding the underlying limestone into the Jebel Akhdar, and exposing the oceanic crust and its covering of deep-sea sediments to wide-spread erosion. In the Jebel Akhdar area can now be seen the high peaks of

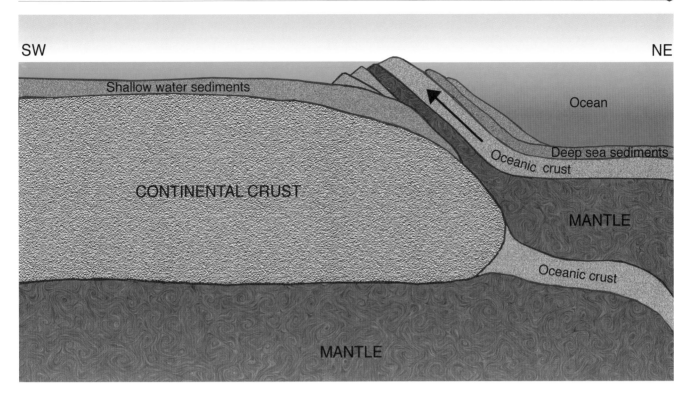

The diagrams show in schematic form how the Hajar mountains came into being. A sheet of oceanic crust pushed over the shallow margin of Oman, taking with it associated deep water sediments. Later the compression and uplifting of the continental crust raised these rock layers more than 10,000 feet, exposing them to continuous erosion for the last 50 million years. The thick black line on the diagram below shows the profile of the land today; the rock layers above the line have been eroded out.

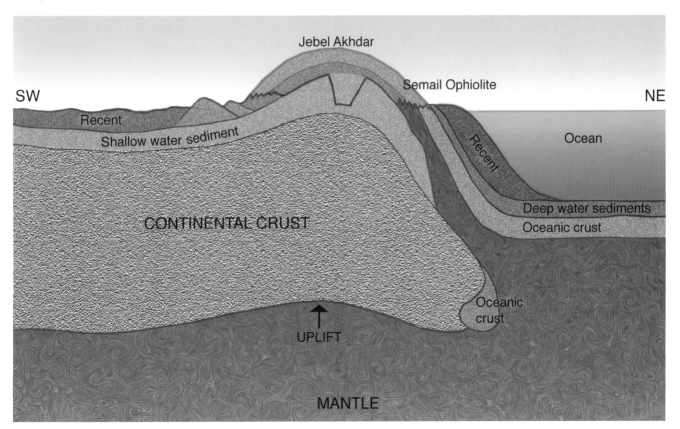

shallow water limestone, the dark reddish shales of the deep-water sediments which once covered the oceanic crust, and the remains of the igneous crust itself, with its basalts, gabbro and pillow lavas better exposed than anywhere else in the world. The dark oceanic crust rocks are known as the Semail Ophiolite.

This remarkable geological sequence distinguishes Northern Oman from the rest of the Arabian peninsula: the colours and land-forms are quite different, and frequently very scenic, with the pale high limestone mountains towering over the dark contorted rocks on either side.

On the other side of Arabia there were forces at work which resulted eventually in the opening of the Red Sea. About 60 million years ago the crust underneath western Arabia thinned and stretched, reducing its structural integrity and causing a series of faults to develop along a line running from Harrat Hadan, which lies east of Taif, north to Jordan. The land along this line slumped and a chain of lakes formed, which during the Palaeocene epoch became a continuous fault-bounded seaway stretching north to join the Mediterranean. Sediments have been found under Harrat Hadan and other *harrats* further north which contain fossils of creatures from that time, which would have lived in both marine and estuarine environments. They include crocodiles, sharks, catfish, lungfish and turtles.

The same crustal thinning process caused a further series of faults some ten million years later, further to the west. Centred on the Bab el Mandab, in the south of the Red

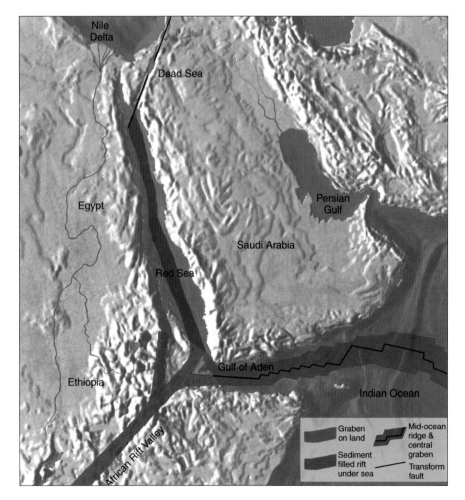

Left: The triple fault radiating from the area of Djibouti. The Great Rift Valley of east Africa appears not to be developing into a spreading edge, whereas the Red Sea and Gulf of Aden rifts are actively widening.

Above: *Pushing through a fault in the old crystalline rocks of the western Shield, a paler coloured dyke is a remnant of a later burst of magmatism.*

Sea, three fracture lines developed. One ran south through east Africa, where the Great Rift Valley now is; one ran east from Djibouti to form the Gulf of Aden; and the third ran northwest where the Red Sea now is. The Red Sea fault was about 100 kilometres wide and 2000 kilometres long; when the sides of the fault separated the central mass fell, resulting in a valley with steep escarpment sides and a broad relatively flat bottom.

At first the valley was not so deep as to connect with the sea. There was a chain of lakes in the deepest part. But as the rifting process continued the northern end of the rift connected with the Mediterranean, which invaded south along the line of the depression. The Red Sea was then for the first time a sea, although there was as yet no link with the Indian Ocean; the land bridge across the southern valley floor still connected Arabia with Africa near Djibouti. Fossils of marine seashells and other creatures identical to Mediterranean fossils of the same period (about 40 million years ago) have been found in the Shumaysi deposits south of Jeddah, demonstrating this ancient link.

Despite the sea that now lay between, Arabia and Africa were still two parts of the same tectonic plate. The great valley had weakened the link, but nothing had yet happened to make the separation final. Continental crust still abutted continental crust. The valley continued to widen, with great slabs of the side walls sliding down into the valley floor. The fault lines along the valley sides provided an easy route for many eruptions of magma pushing up from the mantle, solidifying as they reached the surface to create long thin dykes of basalt and other igneous rocks in numerous places along the foothills of the escarpment sides.

Then, about 25 million years ago, a more fundamental breach was made. Along the centre line of the valley floor a second rift opened, a rift within a rift. This time it was narrow but deep, averaging 1,000 metres but in places 2,000 metres below sea level to the floor of the trench. There was now continuing access to the surface of the earth for mantle material, since the continental crust of the two sides had been for the first time completely severed. The trench floor was made of basaltic magma, flowing up from the mantle along the length of the rift. Each year the trench grew a little wider, a few centimetres annually on average, but made in fits and starts along the line of the trench. Now Arabia began very gradually to rotate anti-clockwise away from Africa, and continued to do so for ten million years, the deep central trench widening as it did so. Along the sides of the valley, where the Tihama plain meets the foothills of the mountains, many intrusions of different kinds of magma created veins and dykes in the older rock.

This dramatic break in the Afro-Arabian continent then slowed and stopped about 15 million years ago (a time when the full thickness of the Arabian plate abutted

Tension begins to pull plate apart. Crust thins and rises. Fault lines develop.

Series of faults develop, blocks of land rift and sink, crust thins further. Volcanism starts parallel to rift.

Rift valley widens, evaporites and other sediments build up in valley. Sea connected to Mediterranean.

Plate finally separates, deep central trench opens and widens. Mountains created as Western Arabia rises.

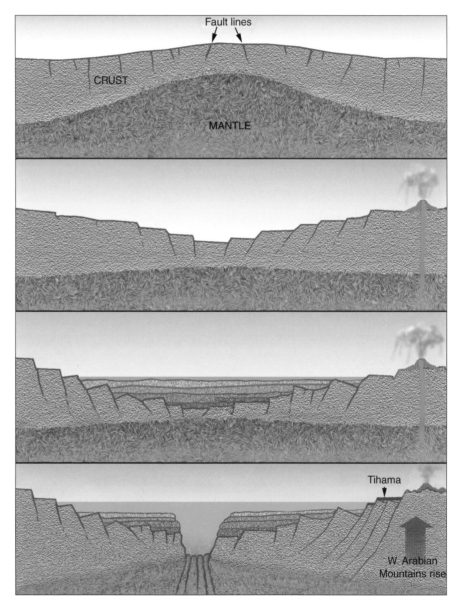

against Eurasia). The gap no longer widened; instead, the whole region gradually swelled, pushed upwards by magma invading the crust. Along the crest of this swelling and running in a north-south direction inland from the Red Sea, a succession of volcanoes erupted when the pressure of the upwelling magma could no longer be contained. This volcanic activity has been more or less continuous for the last ten million years.

The volcanoes are in most cases not picture-book volcanoes; their cones are low and broad, with gently sloping sides, of the type known as "shield" volcanoes from their distant resemblance to an upturned shield. They take this shape because the lava which poured from them was a very fluid basalt which ran easily from the crater or vent and spread out in a broad sheet to cover wide areas far from the crater. In total, these basalt sheets cover more than 150,000 square kilometres of western Saudi Arabia and Yemen, and represent one of the most inhospitable terrains in the country. In general, the southern *harrats*, as these lava-covered regions are called, are older

Below: *High in the mountains between Madina and Yanbu, a remnant of a basalt sheet covers the metamorphic hills near Hima Fiqrah. The dark blackish rock, and the columnar cliffs are both typical of basalt, which can cool into high hexagonal columns.*

HARRAT AREAS

Harrats *cover wide tracts of of the Shield in a rough line parallel to the Red Sea. The map shows their extent. Each harrat consists of many separate basalt sheets, overlain one on another, the results of thousands of individual volcanic eruptions.*

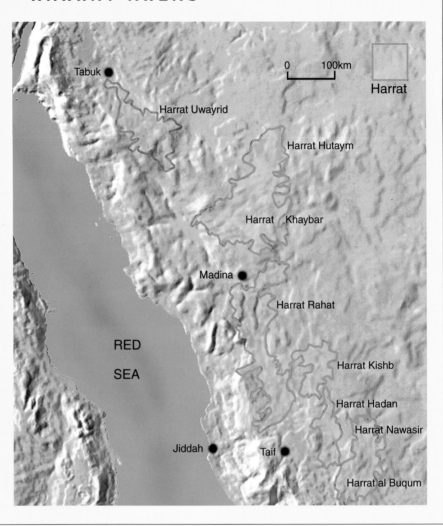

Tabuk

Harrat Uwayrid

Harrat Hutaym

0   100km

Harrat

Harrat   Khaybar

Madina

Harrat Rahat

RED

SEA

Harrat Kishb

Harrat Hadan

Harrat Nawasir

Jiddah   Taif

Harrat al Buqum

Right: *The edge of a* harrat *flow. The way in which the lava folded just before it cooled and solidified is still very apparent.*

than those further north, but most have layer upon layer of basalt built up over millions of years. It is most unlikely that they have reached their final extent even now: there have been 13 eruptions in the last 4,500 years in one northern part of the Harrat Rahat alone, extending some miles south from the holy city of Madina.

The most recent of these occurred only 730 years ago, when earthquakes shook the city of Madina and a sheet of molten basalt poured towards the city. For two days it looked as though the city would be engulfed. The city of Herculaneum in Italy was drowned in just such a sea of flowing volcanic lava in 79 A.D., but Medina was spared the same fate; the flowing river of basalt passed five miles from the city. The cooled black wall of this lava flow can be clearly seen today from the road leading west out of the city towards Qassim. Another earlier recorded eruption occurred 1344 years ago, when a smaller eruption lit up the night sky to the south of Madina. Their frequency in the last few thousand years can be roughly deduced by examining an area known to have been occupied by Neolithic peoples who left on the surface of the basalt many traces of their settlement, including stone tombs or tumuli, stone circles and walls: these monuments are of course absent from more recent flows, assisting geologists to conclude that lava fields which cross over the flows containing neolithic structures must be younger than the end of the neolithic age. It is entirely likely that further eruptions will take place in the future.

The regional uplift which preceded the harrat activity also raised the level of the Red Sea valley floor, turning it into alternating shallow sea and salt lake. Under a hot sub-tropical sun the evaporation rate of these waters was high. The salts and dissolved minerals picked up by rivers and streams running into the sea were precipitated out, building up thick layers on the valley floor. Underlying more recent sediments on the Red Sea floor there is a layer of evaporite salts – halite, gypsum, anhydrite and others – reaching in places a thickness of three kilometres, which dates from this time; as there is also in the Mediterranean.

Below left: Ringed by the dark cliffs of the explosion crater at Wahba, the crater bottom has built up a thick sediment of evaporite salts, such as floored the Red Sea before it became a permanent seaway. The ridges which divide the salt into irregular polygons are typical of these salt expanses. Wahba lies 250 kilometres north-east of Jeddah.

Below: From ancient times salt has been a prized commodity. In central Arabia there are deposits of rock salt which have been mined for sale. Here, a salt vendor in Qassim in north-central Arabia stands beside slabs of good quality rock salt.

Bottom: Desert roses, as these gypsum formations are called, form in damp conditions underground; occasionally the conjunction of the crystals gives a very close resemblance to the petals of a rose.

THE FARASAN ISLANDS

The Farasan Islands are the largest island group in the Red Sea. They lie 40 kilometres off the Tihama coast of Saudi Arabia opposite Jizan, and are low-lying, scarcely rising in some places to 200 feet above sea level. They are surrounded by hundreds of square kilometres of shallow water, frequently only a few metres deep,which cover an extensive area of coral reef. The islands themselves were originally a part of this under-water reef. Like many of the coastal areas in the Red Sea, this area too has been fractured by minor faults – part of the long collapse of the overall Red Sea fault.

About two million years ago this part of the reef was lifted above sea level by a column of salt, known as a *diapir*, pushing its way to the surface from deep underground. The Miocene epoch was an age when long periods of evaporation from a shallow sea or *sabkha* created deep thicknesses of salt sediment below the Red Sea. Strata of salt can, when under pressure from overlying rock, become unstable and start to flow. They will find the path of least resistance to the surface, perhaps using a fault line, raising and pushing aside the overlying rock. The Farasans are an example of this phenomenon.The very rough topography of the islands is partly a result of the surface rocks being pushed aside and contorted by the rising salt, and partly the consequence of the many small fault lines which criss-cross the islands.

Around the coasts are signs of where older beaches have existed, steps cut by waves into the strata above today's shoreline. The fact that these are not uniformly parallel around the islands, as they would normally be, suggests that the upward pressure from the rising salt plug is continuing today, with different areas subject to varying degrees of uplift.

There are other examples of diapirism, as this phenomenon of rising salt columns is called, in Saudi Arabia. The Dammam Dome in Eastern Province is one well-known example. Further examples occur in the central plains of Oman, the most famous being the Qarat al Kabrit, a jagged circle of different rocks which has burst through the otherwise featureless plain.

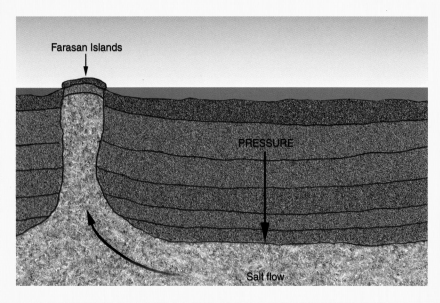

Thick layers of salt can form weaknesses in the crust. Under pressure from overlying rocks it can move like a fluid resulting in faulting of the rock above. It can flow up to the surface, pushing aside the rocks above it, which then show as distorted or anomalous features on the surface. The Dammam Dome in Eastern Province, and the Farasan Islands in the Red Sea are examples of this phenomenon.

The second phase of the Red Sea widening started about five million years ago, when the deep central trench was reactivated. A number of interconnected events then together put in place a Red Sea more recognisable to us today. The Isthmus of Suez rose, cutting the Red Sea off from the Mediterranean; the Gulf of Aden and the Straits of Mandab sank, allowing the Red Sea and Indian Ocean to form a continuous waterway; and there was a renewed rise in the level of the escarpment and adjacent land, which pushed the mountains of Yemen and the Asir Mountains up to their present heights and increased the tilt of the peninsula from west to east. The central deep trench along the mid-line of the Red Sea again started to split, and has continued to do so to the present day. On average it has spread at a rate of about 3 centimetres a year ever since. This may appear to be a leisurely pace, even an insignificant one: but as a result the central Red Sea has widened by 150 kilometres in this last 5-million-year phase of sea-floor spreading.

While we cannot yet tell whether the Red Sea will eventually become a wide ocean, it may well do so. The Atlantic Ocean started in the same way about 170 million years ago, rifting along fault lines similar to the Red Sea fault, at the time of the break-up of the super-continent Pangaea. The important determinant of whether such a rift will turn into a continental break-up seems to be the speed with which the crust stretches; speed is essential, otherwise the lower crust cools as it stretches, and so never thins enough to permit the continuous invasion of magma. Geologists believe that the Great Rift Valley in Africa, for example, will not split further, for this reason.

One interesting light which study of the Red Sea has shed is on the making of the world's continental shelves. The edges of most continents do not plunge steeply down from the coast to the ocean depths. Instead they have broad and relatively shallow margins, which slope down to deep water some tens or hundreds of kilometres offshore. It is not entirely clear why this should be the case, but if the Red Sea is typical of new continental margins then we can understand how they may come about. The initial slump or depression in the land along the line of the future rift creates a wide low-lying shelf which will become the continental shelf of the future continent. So the shallow Red Sea between the Arabian shore and the start of the deep trench some 100 kilometres offshore will one day perhaps represent part of the continental shelf of Asia.

A deep central trench such as the Red Sea has acquired seems to be another typical feature of the world's oceans. The continuous slow addition of new magma material into the trench is the main mechanism for widening the oceans. These deep trenches are also one of the main crucibles for concentrating the world's metals into usable ore-bodies.

In normal circumstances metals such as copper, manganese and gold are very thinly diffused in rocks; much too thinly to be mined economically. Circulating in cracks in the cooling magma at the trench centre is brine – sea-water that has picked up additional salts from the cooling rock. The hot brine is an effective agent in dissolving minute grains of gold and other metals which are carried by convection up to vents in the sea floor, where they cool and discharge their dissolved metals around the mouths of the vents. Over time these can build up to rich ore-bodies. This process is observed to be happening in the brine deeps of the Red Sea, 1000 metres below the surface.

The tectonic events which remoulded the edges of Arabia and gave it its present shape took place over a fifty-million-year time span. The interior of the peninsula was stable throughout that time, changed only by the appearance of the *harrats* on the west and by an increasing tilt of the plate from west down

AQUIFERS

The Arabian Shelf and other areas surrounding the Shield comprise numerous layers or strata of varied sedimentary rock. Each of these strata has its own particular characteristics which determine the type of aquifer it will be. Porosity is important. If for example a sandstone consists of large loosely cemented grains of sand, it will hold more water, and allow that water to flow more freely, than a tight fine-grained sandstone. Some types of rock are impermeable – clay is an example – and may not allow the passage of any appreciable quantities of water. Water enters a rock formation in or near the area where the rock crops out above ground. It will then tend to flow down the gradient of the stratum and, if confined by impermeable strata, will remain in that stratum indefinitely until released naturally by a fault or sinkhole, or artificially by a well. Faults in the strata near Hofuf allow the water in the underlying Umm ar Radhuma formation to flow upwards through the Rus impermeable layer and mix with the water from the Neogene and Dammam aquifers in the Ahsa springs.

Arabia has nine principal aquifers. Six of these are in older sandstone formations, three in limestone. Besides the main aquifers there are numerous smaller ones, some of which are locally important. Between them these aquifers hold a colossal quantity of water, probably to be counted in the hundreds of billions of cubic metres. Over the last fifty years the oil industry has come to understand the underground geology of the country's sedimentary rocks very thoroughly; this knowledge, allied to the rapid advances in the technology of drilling, has enabled these water reserves to be tapped. Their discovery and exploitation has transformed the agricultural life of the country, and made possible the enormous increase in water consumption in the towns and cities. But, rather like oil exploitation, this is not entirely straightforward, and there are problems to be overcome. Firstly, water is not always where it is most needed: substantial reserves under the Rub' Al Khali are not presently of much value, for instance. Secondly, it is mineralised to different degrees, sometimes so much as to make it only marginally useful unless treated first. Even in the same aquifer mineralisation differs substantially from place to place, frequently increasing in mineralisation downslope from the outcrop. In the Biyadh aquifer, for instance, water quality is excellent under the Nisah area, quite good in the Al Kharj area, but very poor in the Eastern Province. Care is also needed in exploiting an aquifer. Some wells are drilled to over 5,000 feet in depth, which involves a substantial investment. Before pumping starts it is essential to establish an accurate sustainable flow rate, which is a function of the aquifer reserves and the porosity of the rock. If this is ignored the well will dry up temporarily until the water level is restored by infiltration from the surrounding rock, and silting or other problems may ensue.

The water in these aquifers is old. Carbon dating of water samples has shown much of the water to be between 15,000 and 25,000 years old, with some much older than that. The further the water is from the outcrop, the older it is. Thus

Above: *Mile after mile of serried date palms make Al Ahsa the greatest oasis in Arabia. The oasis, a corner of which appears in the photograph, has always depended on the steady supply of water from the aquifers which come*

naturally to the surface in the oasis. The water extracted today in Al Ahsa fell as rain more than 15,000 years ago over the western Summan and has travelled very slowly down the slope to the oasis since that time.

while there is quite young water near the outcrop of the Umm ar Radhuma and Dammam formations, the estimated age of water coming out of those formations at Hofuf, 200 kilometres east of the outcrop, is about 18,000 years. Recharge of the aquifers in today's arid climatic conditions is relatively little, so usage constitutes essentially the mining of a fossil reserve. The concern of the Ministry of Agriculture and Water to oversee the proper exploitation of water reserves is a reflection of the finite nature of the resource.

Wadis throughout Arabia tend to be floored with thick layers of sand, gravel and soil. For most of the period since the Pleistocene rainfall has been sufficient to cause both side and main wadis to flow intermittently, carrying debris with the flow, but not sufficient to carry this debris and silt to the sea. As the river flows die out in mid-course the silt is deposited in the wadi bed; and so the thickness of the wadi floors has gradually increased, creating a good water-bearing environment in the process. Wadi deposits are generally very loose and porous; water sinking into them will move easily downstream along the bedrock beneath. Most wells in central Arabia, and many elsewhere, have traditionally been sunk into wadi deposits. Most will not yield much water compared to the rock aquifers described above, but in the days when water was drawn by hand or by animal power they sufficed to water animals or supply villages with their domestic needs. Many have now fallen out of use, but remain an attractive and distinctive feature of country architecture. Sometimes carefully stone-lined, and usually equipped with a superstructure to support rope pulleys made of wood, they are reminders of the simpler, harder lifestyle which predated the introduction of the drilling rig and the diesel pump.

NAME	DESCRIPTION OF AQUIFER
Saq Cambrian	Ordovician sandstone with good quality water. Extends from Tabuk to Buraidah and northeast to the border with Iraq. Very deep towards the northeast.
Wajid Cambrian	Ordovician sandstone, with good quality water. Borders the southeast edge of the Arabian Shield, extending east between Wadi Dawasir and the border with Yemen.
Tabuk	Ordovician sandstone, with fairly good quality water. Overlies the Saq aquifer. Supplies water to Tabuk and Qassim.
Minjur	Coarse triassic sandstone, with fair quality water. A prolific aquifer supplying Riyadh, Kharj and Sudair areas. Wells down to 2000 metres, with water at 60°C. Extends both north and south of central area.
Wasia/Biyadh	Cretaceous sandstone overlying easterly part of Minjur and extending over whole of eastern Arabia. Prolific aquifer with variable quality water.
Umm ar Radhuma	Palaeocene limestone overlying the Wasia/Biyadh aquifers. Variable quality, good in Al Ahsa with large reserves. Extends throughout eastern Arabia.
Dammam	Eocene limestone and marl. Quality and quantity are moderate. Useful in Al Ahsa, the east coast and Wadi Sahba.
Neogene	Various rock types, mainly limestone, of Miocene and later dates. A variable aquifer in terms of water quality and dependability, believed to interconnect with Dammam and Umm ar Radhuma aquifers at some points, notably Al Ahsa.

towards the east. But the normal processes of erosion and sedimentation continued. All the earlier strata east and north of the Dahna sand belt were covered with thick strata of alternating marine and terrestrial sediments. The sea flooded eastern Arabia for several long intervals during this time, but the rocks show that these transgressions became less invasive and lasted for shorter periods as the Tertiary period wore on.

The rocks themselves tell the story. The early Tertiary strata are limestone, but alternate later with sand, clay, marl and sandstone, showing the different environments in which they were deposited. The fossil evidence is also striking. In the Eocene period, between 40 and 50 million years ago, when the sea reached inland as far as the Dahna sand belt, a rich sub-tropical marine fauna lived in the shallow waters. As the strata erode today the hard fossils of these creatures emerge on the surface. The teeth of fish, sharks and rays are excellently preserved, as are sea-urchin spines and various gastropods and

Below: Bony plates from the mouths of two Eagle Rays. These plates were used instead of teeth to crush and grind the molluscs which formed a large part of the diet of these fish. The specimens are Eocene, and work out of the soft sandy deposits in the central Eastern Province.

Below left: Sharks have skeletons of cartilaginous material, not bone, so their skeletons are rarely preserved. Their teeth are the animals' most enduring part, and are common in shallow water marine sediments. These 20 million year old examples come from a number of different species. The specimen at top left is a Hemipristis species; second from right at the top is a Lamner species; the rest are from the Odontaspis family.

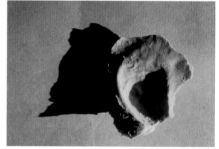

bivalves. At least four species of sharks have been identified from their teeth, including ancestral forms of porbeagle, sand shark, tiger shark and snaggletooth shark. In the Yemen, fossil seeds from this time have been analysed; they reveal that Yemen was then covered in a lowland tropical evergreen forest, and we may imagine that the same vegetation stretched north into Saudi Arabia and east through Dhofar across Oman.

The Miocene epoch, which dawned about the same time as the Red Sea deep central trench first opened, has left behind evidence of the rich terrestrial fauna in the east of the country and in the United Arab Emirates. Fossils of rodents and various cloven hoofed species (artiodactyls) have been located near the Dammam Dome at Jabal Midra ash Shamali, dating from about 23 million years ago. Contemporaneous with those was a new species of mammal, the Masritherium, bones of which have been found near Jizan on the Red Sea

Above: Many bivalves (shells with two parts joined by a hinge of muscle) are found in the fossil record of Arabia, each subtly different. This ostrea latimarginata is common in Miocene deposits in the Eastern Province of Saudi Arabia near Sarrar, and is recognisable by the broad flat edge of the shell.

Opposite: A million years ago, the Arabian shield coursed with rivers. Most of today's wadis were formed at this time. Here we see the ancient river Sahba flowing lazily eastwards down Wadi Nissah near present-day Riyadh, amidst dense vegetation.

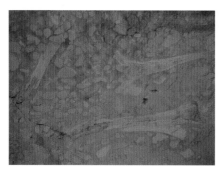

Above: *Part of the cave ceiling reveals a jumble of large mammal bones.*

Top left: *The soft limestone of this hill in the Eastern Summan covers what was once the site of a sluggish estuary. The roof of the shallow cave is dense with the bones of a wide variety of Miocene animals. Presumably a slow current eddied the dead animals into a corner of the lagoon and covered them with a layer of limy silt where they have been preserved.*

Top right: *In the same area as the cave can be seen the tusks of mastodons embedded in the limestone. The mastodon was a forerunner of today's elephant.*

coastal plain in a wadi bank. This large browsing animal, now extinct, resembled a hippopotamus, and must have lived along the lush river margins of the Tihama.

Later on in the Miocene, about 6-8 million years ago, when much of Africa, Eurasia and Arabia, by now all connected with land bridges, were dominated by savannah grasslands, there was a surge of mammal species adapted to this environment, such as early types of giraffe, elephant, cattle and antelopes, as well as predators such as the sabre-toothed tiger and hyaenid types. Fossil bones of these animals have all been found in Abu Dhabi, and many have also been located in Saudi Arabia. The Saudi Arabian relics, at Dabtiyah, Sarrar, Al Jadidah and elsewhere in Eastern Province, are somewhat earlier than those found in Abu Dhabi, and date from the Middle Miocene.

At Dabtiyah were also found skeletal remains of an early hominoid. The descent of man is still a subject which rouses fierce academic controversy, as so much speculation must bridge the wide gaps in the sparse fossil record. The Dabtiyah hominoid is far back in the primate lineage and certainly bore little outward resemblance to modern man; it was part of a branch of the primate tree known as the dryopithecines, and resembled other dryopithecines such as the African *proconsul nyanzae*.

The Sarrar fauna is particularly interesting; it shows fish, crabs, sharks, rays and other creatures living in a river or shallow tidal environment, and also many different land-based vertebrates. These range from snakes, lizards and gerbils up to the largest browsing mammals such as rhinoceros, mastodon and giraffe. Given the mix of species in this fossil graveyard it is most likely that the location was at the time the broad estuary of a river flowing into a tropical or sub-tropical lagoon, fringed with palm trees (a palm trunk was among the fossil remains discovered) and mangroves.

CHAPTER FOUR

❖

MAN UPON THE SCENE

The last major tectonic development of the Arabian plate occurred about three million years ago in the middle of the Pliocene age, resulting in three significant changes to the land. Compression forces along the line where the Arabian and Eurasian plates had collided squeezed the land upwards, raising the Zagros mountains to their present height; the Arabian peninsula was tilted, up towards the southwest and down towards the northeast, which had the effect of depressing the

Three great rivers drained most of the peninsula in the Pliocene period, from 3 mya to 1 mya. Their catchment areas were extensive. During this period of prolonged and heavy rainfall they were probably the equal of today's river Nile. The surface of Northeast Arabia and much of the Empty Quarter consists of their former deltas.

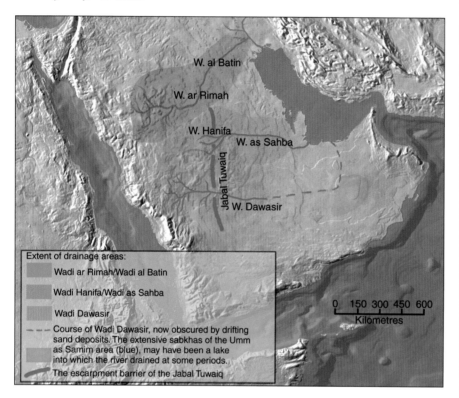

W. al Batin

W. ar Rimah

W. Hanifa

W. as Sahba

Jabal Tuwaiq

W. Dawasir

Extent of drainage areas:

Wadi ar Rimah/Wadi al Batin

Wadi Hanifa/Wadi as Sahba

Wadi Dawasir

- - - Course of Wadi Dawasir, now obscured by drifting sand deposits. The extensive sabkhas of the Umm as Samim area (blue), may have been a lake into which the river drained at some periods.

The escarpment barrier of the Jabal Tuwaiq

0   150 300 450 600
        Kilometres

eastern edge below sea level, creating the Arabian Gulf; and in the Eastern Province the pressure caused by the latest compaction against Asia folded the sedimentary strata in a series of gentle north to south parallel folds, which became the traps for the world's most prolific oilfields.

Contemporary with these geological events was a fundamental change in the region's weather pattern. For the last time a long age of hot wet weather set in over the peninsula, and was to endure for the next two million years. The high rainfall over this extended period changed the Arabian land form in an enduring way. All the land to the east of the Red Sea mountain watershed was scoured by great and powerful rivers; truly prodigious quantities of rock, sand and gravel were carried eastwards to fill in the Rub al Khali basin and to form the wide gravel plains of east and northeast Arabia. Rainfall draining east from the mountains of Yemen created the great Wadi Hadhramant. Although a million years have passed since they regularly flowed along their lengths, the

ARABIA, LAND OF RIVERS

Between three and one million years ago, a regime of high rainfall prevailed over Arabia. Three rivers comparable in size and flow to the world's great rivers of today flowed from west to east across the land, draining into the Arabian Gulf. Their beds, now dry wadis, remain. The broken topography of the western mountains is a result of the eroding power of the water, which carried the debris from the Shield far to the east, through breaks which the rivers carved in the Tuwaiq escarpment barrier.

The Wadi Dawasir pushed through the escarpment at Sulayyil and filled the Rub al Khali depression over a wide area with sand, gravel and rock from the Shield. The Wadi Sahba drained central Arabia, collecting waters from tributaries flowing through the Tuwaiq at Wadi Birk, Wadi Hawtah, and Wadi Nissah before pushing east from Al Kharj to Haradh. Wadi Rumah drained much of the north, flowing northeast towards the Gulf at Kuwait along the Wadi Batin.

Both Wadi Sahba and Wadi Rumah/Batin created vast deltas at their mouths. The Wadi Sahba delta extended from Haradh to the Gulf, over 200 kilometres away, with a width extending from Al Uqair to below Qatar, an arc of over 150 kilometres. Wadi Rumah's delta is now the vast level gravel plain of Dibdibah, which covers much of northeast Arabia around Kuwait.

The gravel in these plains today reveals the power of the rivers. Rounded by tumbling in the river beds, the pebbles comprise every diferent stone in the Shield. Basalt from the *harrats*, granite, diorite, quartz and many others lie mixed together.

When the permanent flow of the rivers ceased one million years ago at the start of the Pleistocene the river beds gradually filled in with debris. This process, called aggradation, happens when brief rains wash sediment into wadi beds, but are too localised or temporary for rivers to carry the sediment far downstream. The river drains into the subsoil, the flow ceases, and the sediment is added to the wadi bed, gradually filling it in. For example, the original river bed of the Wadi Dawasir, where it cuts through the Tuwaiq ecarpment at Sulayyil, lies now 60 metres below the present surface of the wadi; the thick gravel layer which now fills the wadi has been gradually deposited over the last million years by temporary flows of the river, which has not flowed strongly enough to carry it beyond.

Top left: *The only river today in Central Arabia flows for a short distance from the outskirts of Riyadh through the village of Al Hair and thence eastward towards Al Kharj. It follows the route of one small tributary of the great river which once flowed east to the Arabian Gulf through Wadi Sahbah.*

Above left: *Erosion carries rock particles down from higher levels and deposits them when the force of the water subsides, thus forming flat floodplains in valley bottoms. Changes in rainfall patterns can alter the way erosion and deposition operate. Here, the terrace of silt and gravel which has been cut into a former floodplain indicates the change to a regime of lesser rainfall overall. The granite buttresses of Ibn Huwail tower in the background.*

Left: *Sporadic rainfall in most of Arabia means that no permanent rainfed rivers exist in most of the peninsula. Here, a sharp thunderstorm in early spring has filled Wadi Atshanat with a temporary flow which will be dry within a week. The flow is sufficient to carry a little sediment down from the valley sides but will deposit it in the wadi bed when the flow subsides, thus little by little filling up the wadi bed with silt and gravel.*

river beds are still obvious. Most of today's wadis were formed at that time.

The climate was not only very wet in late Pliocene and early Pleistocene times, it was also hot. A heavy sub-tropical forest cover must have blanketed much of Arabia, with a fauna resembling the fauna which now inhabits central Africa. But eventually, just over a million years ago, the world's weather patterns changed again and ushered in a cooler, drier climate in Arabia and in Europe, the start of the long series of glaciations and ice ages. Despite temporary highs and lows since then this pattern has remained to this day. The land became less thickly forested; grass plains became a more typical feature of the landscape, and the fauna populations changed and adapted to the new conditions. This landscape, predominantly savannah wood- and grass-land, was the sight which greeted the first man to step onto the Arabian stage.

In the north of Arabia, at Shuwayhitiyah near Sakaka, is a scatter of stone choppers, cleavers and other implements, made of quartzite, which lie along the banks of a wadi. These tools are considered to date from almost one million years ago. They are not spectacular to look at, nor very beautiful, and to the untrained eye appear little different from the mass of broken stones which litters the valley floor. But they are some of the oldest stone tools outside Africa and mark the place where a group of the first human ancestors stopped for a period on their journey out of Africa, during man's early spread across the world. They are significant because such early sites are so rare. They represent the earliest record of man's adaptation to his service of the geology of Arabia.

Another assemblage of similar tools has been found in the south of the country near Najran, which may belong to the same culture, but there is relatively little evidence of widespread populations of these earliest people, who may have been few in number.

Who were these first men in Arabia? No fossil skeletons have yet been found, so we must rely on the stone tools to tell us. We can make an informed deduction as to their identity by comparing the Shuwayhitiyah finds with others from a site which not only has similar types and styles of tool, but also fossil bones of the toolmakers. The largest and best researched such site is at Olduvai Gorge, in Tanzania. Olduvai is a narrow gorge which cuts through sedimentary deposits laid down over the last two million years; in the sediments on the sides of the gorge are exposed, layer upon layer, the evidence of man's earliest use of stone tools. Painstaking research has shown how the tools changed over time, with the deposits being analysed by potassium argon and other sophisticated techniques to give a time scale for these changes. The Shuwayhitiyah tools resemble very closely those in the Upper Olduvan layers, which date from just over a million years ago. The makers of these artefacts were an ancestral species of human known as *homo erectus*. This early man was short, strongly built, with a brain size only two thirds as large as the modern human brain; his face had heavy brow ridges over the eyes, powerful jaws but a weakly developed chin. He lived as a hunter and gatherer. Fossils of *homo erectus* are scarce, but have been found in China, Indonesia, Europe and many parts of Africa, showing that he did eventually colonise most areas of the old world; he probably survived until about 150,000 years ago, and over the long period between his arrival at Shuwayhitiyah and his final disappearance from Arabia he left very many traces of his presence, in the form of the stone tools he fashioned and discarded.

Next spread: An andesite dyke runs high above the surrounding plain, providing both a vantage point and a plentiful stone quarry for homo erectus camped in its lee. A lake, a watering place for game, lies nearby. Early man depended on hunting, scavenging and gathering; campsites such as this would have been used only so long as food sources remained plentiful, but may have been a seasonal halt on an established annual circuit. Today a litter of worn chipped stones on the desert surface is the only reminder of the life of those early men.

At Shuwayhitiyah and Najran the tools are very crudely made. The maker selected a suitable cobble stone of quartzite, then with another stone used as a hammer struck off a few flakes from the surface of the cobble until he was left with the shape he desired. There are about a dozen principal shapes, which would have served different purposes. The principal ones were cleavers and scrapers used for butchering, picks for digging up roots and tubers, and bifaces, which were general purpose tools. They were rough but serviceable objects.

A long gap then appears in the record of habitation of Arabia. This may be, and most likely is, because the evidence of continued occupation has disappeared, buried under more recent sediments. Whatever the reason, in the period after 500,000 years ago there appears a profusion of sites with a new, more highly developed stone-working industry. These new tools also were made and used by *homo erectus*, but we do not know whether the original Arabian population had learnt the new technology from their fellow men in Africa,where it developed, or whether a new wave of *homo erectus* had swept into Arabia from Africa carrying their new tools with them

By this time the crude original biface, the early all-purpose tool, had been developed into something more useful, which we know as a handaxe. This new tool spread rapidly throughout Africa, Western Europe and South and West Asia, and continued in use until it was supplanted by a different technology less than 100,000 years ago. Its essential form did not change over that time: it was oval, pointed at one end, with an edge running down both sides of the tool to the pointed, thinner end. There were of course many variations. Size ranged between 10 and 30 centimetres in length; some were more crudely fashioned than others; they were made from a wide variety of different stones; and some were adapted for particular functions (for example, having a blade rather than a point at the end). But these are all variations on a central theme, an ideal shape, which was for 400,000 years man's principal tool, and which must be the most successful industrial design of all time.

Weighing an average 500 grams, the handaxe was a tool to be held in the hand, without a handle, and was used for cutting, scraping, stabbing, skinning – any task, in fact, which required a blade or a point.

The toolkit comprised numerous other shapes as well as the handaxe. Stone

Above: *A small handaxe of the type found at Saffaqah. The great age of the tool is evident from the worn edges of the flake scars. The hard hammer, stone-on-stone, technique of making it is clear from the deep rounded scars in the stone. But still, the maker would have had a sharp hard and serviceable tool for his use.*

Top left:*A quartzite handaxe showing the long shallow flake scars typical of soft hammer technique. The sharp edge running round the tool is straight, whereas typical hard hammer tecknique would have left a zigzag edge.*

Top right: *Flint develops an opaque whitish skin as it is exposed to weathering. The limace handaxe shown in the photograph has a deeply patinated surface, showing it to be very ancient*

balls, which could have been used for projectiles (but which experimentation has
shown to be more probably hammerstones), heavy bladed cleavers, notches to
shave down wooden shafts for spears, and the flakes themselves, which could be
used for knives. At one site near Dawadmi in Nejd excavators have found many
thousands of tools, made of rhyolite and andesite obtained from nearby outcrops.
These tools are about a quarter of a million years old. The successive strata in
which they were buried show that at certain times some tool shapes and types were
commoner than at other times, which allows informed speculation on changing
conditions and lifestyle. The tools talk. For example, a sudden increase in the
proportion of scrapers and points useful for hide processing suggests a temporary
deterioration in the weather to wetter and colder conditions, when animal skins
would have been in greater demand for clothing and shelter.

From the first, man had learnt to be selective in his choice of material for tools.
Long before he learnt to use language, or control fire, or construct shelters, he had
mastered the art of discriminating between different types of stone. For his tools
he needed stone that was hard, that would not split or crumble easily, that would
take a sharp and lasting edge, and, importantly, that could be flaked predictably.
Most sedimentary rock and many of the coarsegrained types of igneous rock do
not have these properties. Most types of limestone and sandstone are too soft to be
useful. Some granite is too coarse. Schist and slate split too easily. By a process of
trial and error, a short list of suitable stones was found to be useful. Fine grained
igneous rock such as andesite and basalt were popular for their hardness, though
not easy to work. Flint, chert, and the rare volcanic glass, obsidian, were highly
prized for predictable flaking qualities, and the sharpness of the edge they would
take. Metamorphic quartzite was frequently used: today old quartzite tools have
taken on a grayish or brownish tinge, but when new they must have had the
added, aesthetic, merit of being brilliant white or pink. The earliest tools in
Arabia at Shuhaytiyah were made of quartzite.

As man spread through Arabia the habitats he chose were dictated by themes
of water, food and shelter. But an important subsidiary criterion must have been
the availability of suitable stone materials for tools and weapons. Archaeologists
have identified thousands of stone age sites across Arabia, all with a repertoire of
stone tools. The location of many of these sites is clearly based on suitable stone
quarries. As the local geology changes so does the material of the local stone
tools. It is unusual in Arabia to find tools of the Acheulian culture (as the handaxe
culture is more commonly called) more than a day's trek from a quarry or source
area where they might have originated.

Quarries in the Arabian Shield by their nature tend to contain very large
quantities of stone; dykes of andesite, sheets of basalt and hills of granite possess
inexhaustible reserves of rock. In limestone areas such as much of Nejd east of
the Shield the rocks most commonly used were quartzite or quartzose sandstone,
where it outcropped, or flint, which appears in scattered deposits on the eroded
limestone surface. Over wide areas no suitable strata exist, particularly in the
south and east of the country. The flat stretches of the Rub' al Khali and similar
terrain in the northeast offer no suitable bedrock material, being composed of

FLINT

Left *The modern road running west out of Riyadh cuts through a number of sections of limestone as it leaves Riyadh. The photograph shows a view of part of a roadcut in which fresh nodules and lenses of flint have been exposed by the excavators. Notice the dark colour of the freshly exposed flint and the whitish skin or cortex which edges the nodules.*

Flint is a silica, like opal and quartz. It is frequently but erroneously believed to be of igneous origin. In fact it derives from the skeletons of sponges. In the shallow seas in which limestone formed, sponges of many different species thrived. Some sponges (like the well-known bathroom sponge) have flexible protein skeletons; most have hard skeletons composed of opaline silica. The disintegrating skeletons of dead sponges fell to the sea floor and were eventually buried under it. The highly soluble opaline silica dissolved in the groundwater, and was carried in concentration to cavities where it was precipitated in the insoluble form of flint. Where conditions were favourable, these flint deposits grew into lumps, or nodules, or sometimes into large flat sheets.

When limestone formations are exposed to erosion they weather relatively rapidly. Flint is a very hard rock; as the limestone erodes, the flint nodules embedded in it remain on the surface. There, it may be broken by frost or other natural action, and with exposure to the elements will develop a whitish crust, or cortex. The original light-absorbing micro-crystalline structure of the flint makes it appear dark grey or black when fresh; as the structure decays, so it becomes light-reflecting and therefore pale in colour. This phenomenon is helpful in allowing archaeologists to estimate the rough age of flint tools used by early man; the greater the amount of cortex formed on the knapped flint, the older the tool. This is only useful as regards palaeolithic flint tools, since cortex formation takes many thousands of years to develop.

Left: *Sand, gravel and silt cover the Empty Quarter. Here, the last boulders before the sands begin provided a quarry site for ancient man in search of quartzite for his tools. Today they are a home for foxes.*

drifting sand, soft marl and loess, and extensive plains of gravel. There, the only workable stone available was to be found in the water-worn cobble stones carried down from the igneous formations far to the west by the Pliocene river systems, such as Wadi Dawasir and Wadi Sahba. The rounded stones in these ancient river beds originated from throughout the extensive drainage areas of the rivers and thus contain numerous different kinds of rock. Given the scarcity of available suitable stone, it is no surprise that palaeolithic man's tools from these areas are made of the same wide variety of stones – basalt, quartzite, flint, and others. He had to fabricate a large tool such as a handaxe from the relatively small river cobbles available, and exhibited a cleverness in achieving the largest size of tool by carefully removing the minimum number of flakes from the original cobble, leaving a large part of the original surface untouched.

We have remarked on the amazing continuity of this old stone age, or

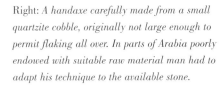

Right: *A handaxe carefully made from a small quartzite cobble, originally not large enough to permit flaking all over. In parts of Arabia poorly endowed with suitable raw material man had to adapt his technique to the available stone.*

palaeolithic, culture, and the conservatism which led these people to produce essentially the same repertoire of tools for hundreds of thousands of years. Certainly man became more skilful or careful in his craftsmanship, sometimes producing very beautiful tools with the stone-on-stone or "hard hammer" technique he used; but he introduced only one fundamental change in manufacturing technique during that long time.

The old technique of hard hammer flaking was gradually superseded for finishing off tools by the "soft hammer" technique. Batons of antler or wood were being used instead of a hammerstone to strike off the final edge flakes, allowing a greater precision both of direction and pressure to be applied to the stone core. As a result, flake scars were less deep and a more precisely symmetrical tool could be made, with a straight and more effective edge in place of the sinuous edge that commonly results from stone-on-stone flaking.

The stone tool culture of early Arabia was replaced by a quite different approach to tool-making sometime after 100,000 years ago. By then *homo erectus* had died out, and been succeeded by a new race known as Neanderthal man. Neanderthals were of heavier build than *homo erectus*; they shared certain physical traits such as prominent bony ridges over the eyes; but in mental capacity they were far advanced, their brain size being at least as great as that of modern humans. We do not know where they originated, though their remains are found throughout Europe, Africa and the Middle East; nor do we know why they should have died out about 35,000 years ago. Modern humans had shared the land with them in most parts of the Middle East for thirty or forty thousand years by then, competing with them for resources. Was the Neanderthal decline due to a gradual marginalisation in the search for food? Were they less aggressive than modern humans? Was their fundamental disadvantage, as some have proposed, that the physical construction of their throat made it impossible for them to develop speech, that faculty which gave modern humans the ability to organise,

Above: *A Levallois core (top left) showing clearly the scars where two triangular points have been struck off.*

Left: *Flint blades struck by Neanderthal man. Note that the upper edge of the middle blade no longer has the brown patination of the other suraces, showing that it was reworked and sharpened long after it was first struck.*

to pass on learning, and to speculate about the past and the future with each other and so to add to the common store of knowledge and understanding? Or did they succumb to some disease to which modern humans were resistant?

In any event, they did disappear, but have left behind in Arabia evidence of their great advance in stone-working. They still used Acheulian techniques for some of their tools, but the important innovation which they introduced to Arabia was the blade tool. They found they could detach a succession of very precise blades from a flint nodule, and so produce many tools from one rock, where Acheulian man would have produced one tool and many discarded flakes. Less effort and fewer raw materials were needed to achieve the same quantity of usable tools. Their blades were long, sharp-edged, and could be made with angles of varying degrees of acuteness. The basic blade could then be modified by further careful soft hammer flaking to create points, borers, burins (a type of chisel), scrapers and other delicate tools.

Another similar technique, which may have first been understood by *homo erectus* but was fully exploited by Neanderthals, was the "Levallois" technique. A core was prepared in such a way that a succession of points or blades of precisely predetermined shape could be then struck off with a single blow. Again, it was an intelligent way both of maximising use of raw material and economising on effort.

All the evidence that remains of Neanderthal occupation of the land are a few dusty sites on rocky jebels and gravel plains, usually associated with outcrops of flint and chert, his favoured materials. We know that these are Neanderthal because the tools lying there are the same tools, the same technology as are found associated with Neanderthal bones elsewhere in western Asia and in Europe.

The sites are scattered thinly throughout western and central Arabia. They probably represent no great density of population, since the period from 70,000 to 35,000 years ago was a time of increasing aridity; progressively shorter wet spells alternating with arid periods in the time up to 50,000 years ago finally gave way to a long period of continuous aridity between 50,000 and 35,000 years ago, probably presenting the inhabitants with harsh living conditions, and an environment where few folk could sustain a reasonably secure life.

Anatomically modern man had already coexisted with Neanderthals in western Asia, sharing the same food resources, for upwards of 30,000 years by the time the Neanderthals vanished. Just at the time when modern man had finally eliminated his rival, conditions became suddenly propitious for him to colonise the land in greater numbers. A sustained wet period, starting about 35,000 years ago and continuing for the next 18,000 years, changed the face of the land. Surface water was abundant, though not sufficient to reactivate wholly the three great ancient rivers, whose channels had long since become choked with sand dunes and other loose sediments. Extensive fresh water lakes in Yabrin, Layla, Al Ahsa, and far to the south in Mundafan and the Ramlat Al Sabatayn, were enduring features of the landscape; woodlands and prairies covered the face of the land; and a resurgence of grazing animals such as buffalo and antelope provided plentiful game for hunters. Hippopotamus browsed in the lakes; tantalising skeletal evidence suggests elephants roamed the land (which would not be too surprising: there is good evidence that Egyptian pharaohs hunted elephant in the Alghab marshes of Syria as recently as 4,000 years ago).

This changed weather pattern was associated with the onset of the last great pulse of Arctic glaciation, which covered the north of Europe, Asia and Canada with immense sheets of ice. So much of the world's water was locked into these ice sheets that sea levels progressively fell. In the early Pleistocene, 1.5 million years ago, world sea levels had been 75 metres above today's level. During the late Pleistocene levels progressively dropped until, at the height of the glaciation, about 20,000 years ago, sea levels were about 100 metres below their present levels. The Arabian Gulf was dry land as far down as the Straits of Hormuz, and one could have walked dry shod from Iran to Dubai, except for the difficulty of crossing the Tigris and Euphrates which flowed down the centre of the Gulf before emptying then into the sea in the Gulf of Oman.

CHAPTER FIVE

FROM STONE TO BRONZE

The same worldwide climatic changes which ended the last ice age in Europe and north Asia and which saw the glaciers retreating and the temperate forests spreading north, had far-reaching effects in Arabia. About 17,000 years ago, the lakes in Yabrin, Layla, Mundafan and the Ramlat al Sabatayn in the south, which had existed since the onset of the great rains 35,000 years ago, dried

Right: *Pleistocene lakebed at the foot of one of the long transverse uruq in the southwest Rub al Khali.*

Right: *Part of the evidence for late Pleistocene and recent climatic shifts is to be found in the dunes themselves. In the Dahna west of Khurais, and in the western Rub al Khali at Mundafan and elsewhere, areas of hard silty mud can be seen at different levels on the dunes. These are relic stretches of the old lakebeds. Some – the older, Pleistocene levels – protrude from the base of the dunes; others, dating from the second wet period, occur high up in today's dunes. Carbon 14 dating of the fresh-water molluscs in these muds enable us to date their formation and their ending.*

The fact that these undisturbed patches of old lakebed exist in the dunes means logically that those dunes themselves have not moved for at least 5000 years. Of course there is movement on the crests, where the wind blows the topmost sands back and forth; but the bulk of the dune mass remains in place. Occasionally a driver on these dunes will be taken unawares by finding a patch of sand so hard that no wheelmark or footprint will register. That may be an exposed patch of Plestocene dune, already cementing in the first stage of transformation into sandstone.

The photograph shows an exposure of hard dry mud at Mundafan, fifty metres above the base of the dune.

up or shrank dramatically, leaving embedded in their dry silt numerous fossil bones of the antelope, buffalo and hippopotamus which had roamed central Arabia. The savannah grassland dotted with forest trees thinned out and died back. With little surface vegetation or root systems to hold it in place, the fertile topsoil and humus desiccated, turned into dust and was blown away in windstorms. Desert conditions at least as inhospitable as those we see today were created.

Once the stabilising topsoil had gone, the underlying sand was mobilised by the winds and shaped into dune systems, creating the vast sand deserts of the Nafud, the Dahna and the Rub al Khali. Many of the dunes created then still

SAND

A distinctive feature of the surface of Arabia is the widespread sheets and belts of mobile sand. A little more than one third of the country is covered by sand, an area of over 700,000 square kilometres.

From the map it will be seen that sand cover is concentrated in five principal areas. By far the largest is the Rub' Al Khali, which is celebrated as the largest continuous area of sand in the world. The Great Nefud in the north is also large, at 60,000 square kilometres. Between these two lie the Dahna, a great arc of dunes running over 1,000 kilometres to join the two sand seas. Distinctive thin dune belts (*Uruq* in Arabic) run down the western edge of

Right: *Marching to the horizon, the long parallel ridges of these dunes lie about 1 kilometre apart and can run upwards of 200 kilometres in length.*

the Tuwaiq escarpment, paralleling the Dahna. Finally, the Jafurah is a block of mobile dunes lying between Hofuf and the Rub' Al Khali to the south. Elsewhere, scattered smaller areas of sand form a patchwork across many parts of the land, from the Red Sea Tihama coast to the rocky wadis of Nejd. Where did this vast quantity of sand come from? The short answer is, from the granite and other coarse-grained igneous rocks of the Shield. As the granite eroded, the bonds holding its component minerals of quartz and feldspar loosened, and the individual crystals broke free as a coarse sand. With time, the softer feldspar abraded into powder to form a basic constituent of dust, clay and loess. The quartz grains, by contrast, retained their size, because quartz is one of the hardest and most durable minerals. Constant abrasion from the erosion process rounded off their angular edges, polished them to some degree, but did not destroy them

Dunes are created by the winds. They can take several distinct shapes, which are governed by the type of sand of which they are made, and by the strength and seasonal direction of the prevailing winds. Where the prevailing wind comes from the same direction throughout the year the dunes will take a form different from those in an area where the wind changes direction seasonally, or where there is no particular prevailing direction to the wind. Because the forces which dictate dune shape tend to be regional in extent so a particular sand region will tend to have one prevailing dune type.

A traveller through the sand regions of Arabia will find an infinite variety of

Left: *North of Wadi Dawasir the closely packed lines of the Uruq al Wadi can present a challenge to the traveller.*

sizes and shapes of dunes in the sandscape. Nonetheless, most fall into one of the following four categories.

Transverse

A terrain which occurs when winds are predominantly from the same direction. The ridges run perpendicular to the wind direction. It consists of long, gently rounded ridges, sometimes with a steep slip face on the lee side; or of crescent-shaped barchan dunes, the convex side pointing into the wind and the concave side, in the lee of the wind, with a steep slip face. Barchan dunes tend to be mobile, their speed of travel depending on the terrain they cross, the extent of humidity and therefore vegetation cover, and wind speed.

The Jafurah is an area where these dune forms predominate. Running south from Abqaiq in a widening band parallel to the coast, the sand here is about 90 % quartz, whereas in the Dahna and most parts of the Empty Quarter it is usually over 97% quartz. The Jafurah is also distinctively pale. In most other sand areas of Arabia the grains have picked up a coating of iron oxide from adjacent sediment, and this rusty coating gives dunes their frequently beautiful reddish or orange colours. The Jafurah typically has a NNW wind, so the ridges, and the barchans horn-to-horn, align in a roughly ENE-WSW direction.

Longitudinal

Various forms of undulating sand sheet, with low to intermediate dune

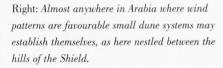

Right: *Almost anywhere in Arabia where wind patterns are favourable small dune systems may establish themselves, as here nestled between the hills of the Shield.*

heights. They are relatively stable and frequently have considerable cover of bushes and grass, particularly in the hollows of the dunes. The common name for this type of terrain is *"dikaka"*.

The Great Nefud is for the most part of this type. It stretches as a forbidding barrier across 300 kilometres of the north of Arabia, between Al Jawf in the north and Hail to the south, and has almost no wells or oases within its 60,000 square kilometre extent. The Palaeozoic sandstone hills immediately to the west suggests a possible source for much of the Nefud's sand.

Sand Mountains

Individual sand peaks, rising up to 1,000 feet from their base. They take very different and irregular shapes. Some are complex, with smaller dunes built high up on their flanks. Others are simple giant barchans, pyramids, or huge domes. There tends to be no strong prevailing wind where they commonly occur.

The most spectacular array of these sand mountains is to be found in the remote southeast corner of the Rub' Al Khali, where each mountain sits isolated from its neighbours on a white *sabkha* plain. Elsewhere, as in the eastern Nefud, they are found with other sand types. One smaller but well-known sand mountain, the "star dune", lies in the middle of the Irq Banban north of Riyadh, its presence perhaps explained by a break in the nearby escarpment which causes wind patterns to swirl irregularly over that spot.

Left: *Parallel to the escarpment of the Tuwaiq for much of its length, and a few kilometres to the west of it, runs a series of narrow sand belts. Here northwest of Sulayyil the dunes of the Nafud ad-Dahi taper off into the outlying hills of the Shield.*

Uruq

This fourth dune type is a long thin line of sand, well defined on both sides, and usually with a sharp crest along the line of the summit. The name suggests the shape: 'irq (of which *uruq* is the plural) means vein, stem, or root in Arabic.

Sometimes these uruq line up in parallel ranges, as in the southwest Rub Al Khali where they represent the dominant form. On average 1.5 to 2 kilometres apart, they run for 200 kilometres on a NE-SW line, perhaps 100 in number. They are believed to be the product of two alternating winds, easterly and northerly; and although they are migrating very slowly southwest, they have certainly been in approximately their present positions for at least 2,000 years. Neolithic man abandoned his implements on these and many other dunes: the fact that they still lie there demonstrates the long relative stability of some dune systems. Elsewhere, uruq are found in parts of the Nefud, in parts of the Dahna (for example, where the Riyadh-Dammam expressway cuts through) and as many isolated sand lines across the country. One lengthy stretch runs a few kilometres west of the Tuwaiq escarpment; another, the 'Irq Banban mentioned above, parallels the Buwaib escarpment north of Riyadh. The Rub' Al Khali includes all of the above types. It covers such a large area that many combinations occur of the variables of wind speed, wind direction, sand supply and underlying sedimentary cover. The result is a great variety of dune forms.

Right: *This typical dune terrain lies in the Great Nefud between Hail and Sakaka.*

This is also true, if to a lesser extent, of the Dahna. These sands are much more accessible and therefore less daunting than the Rub' Al Khali. But since it stretches for 1,100 kilometres, from the Great Nefud to the western Rub' Al Khali, it is one of the principal land features of Arabia. It is as long as the Tuwaiq escarpment. It swings in an arc parallel to and east of the series of Mesozoic escarpments. It has been suggested that its shape derives from a combination of wind direction, sand availability from the old river drainage systems which it crosses (Wadi al Rimah, Wadi Sahba) and the underlying ground structure. Today it is valued as a grazing ground, with spring rains covering its sands with khozama, erymobium and other palatable annal herbs for the flocks that are sent there.

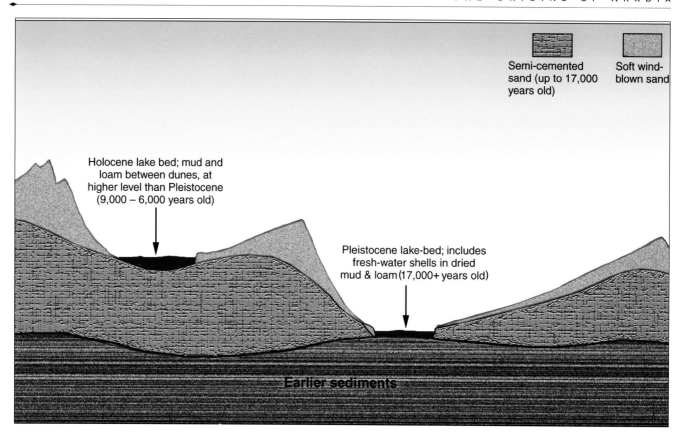

Semi-cemented
sand (up to 17,000
years old)

Soft wind-
blown sand

Holocene lake bed; mud and
loam between dunes, at
higher level than Pleistocene
(9,000 – 6,000 years old)

Pleistocene lake-bed; includes
fresh-water shells in dried
mud & loam (17,000+ years old)

Earlier sediments

Above: A cross-section of parallel irqs *in the Empty Quarter, showing why beds of dry mud can be found at sharply different levels.*

exist today. The effect on the fauna must have been severe, driven into those favoured pockets where perennial water could be found. Man, too, must have migrated away from the increasingly barren land, since he still led a hunter-gatherer existence and could not, as he later could after the domestication of the camel, stray far from a permanent water source.

The return of the rains 9,000 years ago heralded the return of conditions once more favourable to man's colonisation of the land. A further change in the weather systems at that time brought back a wetter climate, in particular to the southern half of the peninsula. The monsoon, which now brings rain only to the extreme south coast of the peninsula in Dhofar, swung north to bring seasonal rain across the Rub' Al Khali. Thick permanent grassland was re-established, the dunes were stabilised and a layer of topsoil covered the sand. Lake beds filled again with water.

This greener Arabia and its abundant wildlife attracted man to expand his presence in the country. The evidence of their settlement has been found in all parts, from the Tihama plain in the west to the shores of the Arabian Gulf. This wave of human activity was characterised by a wholly new stone tool culture known as the neolithic. In Europe and much of the Middle East this new stone tool culture coincided with the introduction of agriculture, but in Arabia the evidence points to its use by hunter-gatherer people for several thousand years before agriculture became common.

We saw earlier how Neanderthals and early *homo sapiens* devised a technique of splitting many blades from a single flint nodule. The great advance in

stoneworking which the neolithic age produced was the development of a
technique called "pressure flaking". By applying a point (of antler, for instance)
to the stone being worked, and then applying pressure until a flake broke off, a
wonderfully precise control was achieved and the inevitable inaccuracies of
hammering techniques were eliminated. But, for this to be successful, it was
necessary to have a stone which flaked predictably. Flint and chert were the
stones of choice, with quartzite commonly used where these were unavailable.
Obsidian a volcanic glass found in a few areas in the Shield and some other rarer
but beautiful stones such as chalcedony could also be flaked predictably, but
formed only a minor component of the neolithic toolkit.

Neolithic man's tools were small and light, worked in a large variety of very
specific shapes to cover the needs of their more complicated and sophisticated
culture. For this was an age of incredible progress. Their tools tell us how these
men lived in much more detail than palaeolithic tools revealed about early man's
lifestyle. Now we find a great variety of shapes and sizes of tool, each with a very
specific function. Gone were the days of clumsy all-purpose tools.

They show us how he caught game. Archery was a normal method of hunting,
and it is clear that he shot birds, small game and larger animals. The arrowheads
that are commonly to be seen on the desert surface range in size from two
centimetres in length, too small to be effective except against birds up to eight
centimetres and more. The wooden bow, the corded bowstring, the arrow shaft
and the sinew which bound the arrowhead to the shaft have all long since
decayed; they are to be seen now only in the engravings on rock faces which

*Above: Knives were made of flint and quartzite.
These quartzite examples show how, as the blades
became blunt with use, they were resharpened by
pressure-flaking along the edge, so that in time the
original thin slightly rounded edge was steepened
and straightened with continual resharpening.*

*Above left: Quartzite stones, battered into spheres,
were once thought to be missiles, but are now
thought more probably to be hammerstones.*

*Top left: At different times man must have found
different ways to attach his arrowheads to the arrow
shaft. The tang, the blunt end of the arrowhead,
takes different forms ranging from long and thin to
short and squat. Occasionally a hollow tang – such
as the one on the left – is found in Arabia`, though
this was a shape more common in Egypt. Each
shape denotes a different attachment method.*

*Top right: Starting with a roughly worked blank of
chert, the neolithic toolmaker has started to
presssure-flake an arrowhead, starting at the point.
Some imperfection in the stone has caused him to
abandon the task. The unfinished arrowhead shows
very clearly the difference in precision between soft
hammer and pressure flaked workmanship.*

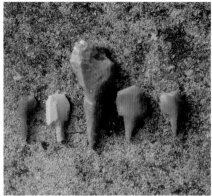

Above: *Knives and scrapers of quartzite lie where they were abandoned thousands of years ago.*

Top left: *Hand grindstones, used for grinding and crushing cereals, were made of different stones. These examples are of sandstone, quartzite and a dark volcanic rock. Given our respect for early man's knowledge of the qualities of different stones, we must assume that these different materials produced – deliberately – different intended results.*

Top middle: *These tiny points were awls, used to pierce hides and make delicate holes in material so that they could be sewn. They help to prove the existence of sewing at a very early date.*

Top right: *Scrapers had been a fundamental part of man's toolkit from the earliest times. In the neolithic age this basic tool started to take on many deliberate forms, including notches of a precise diameter to shave shafts for arrows and spears and many other specific functions. These examples are typical of the variety found.*

these people left behind.

Spearheads, too, are common, and are known in many sizes. Fish hooks are found near old lake beds and by the coast. It seems that these men devised specific means to catch and trap all the various sources of protein available to them.

Man had hitherto been exclusively a hunter and gatherer, who had to follow his food sources – migrating animals, or seasonal fruits and vegetation. Now he learnt to sow cereal crops, domesticating barley and other grains, to be harvested and stored for use throughout the year. There was no longer a need to migrate: settled communities could exist permanently in one place, though the nomadic way of life undoubtedly continued side by side with them. Neolithic settlement sites have an abundance of grindstones and pestles which demonstrate the importance of cereals as a food source to this society, though no doubt there was a long period when collection and preparation of wild cereals preceded their domestication and cultivation. Interestingly, the grindstones they used are in many very varied materials, mainly sandstones, which range in texture from fine to very coarse, suggesting that different stones were used either for different grains or for different stages in the grinding process. This provides further evidence of specialisation.

The variety of tools for scraping, boring and cutting is equally wide. With these, they could process wood and skins very precisely: we can easily believe that fine sewing, woodworking skills and all manner of domestic tasks were within their grasp.

At some stage during this long cultural revolution, perhaps four or five thousand years ago, the neolithic people domesticated the camel and the donkey, and so could travel longer distances on camel or donkey back. One advantage this gave them was the ability to source their stone materials from a much wider radius than had previously been possible. For example, in Jubbah, north of Hail in the Nefud, neolithic tools have been found of chert and rhyolite. The nearest source of chert is in the Aruma limestone outcrop, 140 kilometres northeast of Jubbah; the nearest source of rhyolite is near Hail, 60 kilometres away. They also obviously transported heavier stones. When excavated, the neolithic village at Thumama was found to contain a block of diorite which may have been used as a bench. Diorite is an igneous rock; the nearest diorite source is almost 200 kilometres from Thumama. Why go to the trouble of carrying it all that way?

Above: *A hunting scene showing riders on horseback armed with spears and swords attacking camels. There may have been populations of wild camels in Arabia long after the camel was domesticated, as today there still exist wild Bactrian camels in Central Asia. Pictures such as this tend to confirm such a view.*

Below: *The process of patination is very clear in this picture. The rather crudely drawn camels on the rock at the rear still retain the pale colour of the underlying rock. The much more ancient engraving on the front rock, showing a long-horned piebald cow, has acquired a colour indistinguishable from the rock on which it has been engraved and must be several thousand years old. The climate and vegetation in the Jibal Wajid must have been very different at that time, to have supported cattle.*

Above: *A troop of onagers, or wild asses, have been closely observed and vividly depicted by the engraver. It is remarkable how such early engravings so often reveal a deep understanding of the animal's character.*

Above: *The final development of stone tools was the polished stone axe, chipped and ground to a smooth surface. These small implements which would have been mounted in a haft, were usually made of a hard igneous rock.*

Because they liked the look of the stone, for aesthetic reasons? For practical reasons, as a source of future hard stone tools? A conundrum without a definite answer. That they did have an aesthetic sense is clear. They made stone beads from a variety of decorative stone; they collected fossils of seashells, weathered out of the limestone strata, which could have served no useful purpose but which now lie scattered on their old campsites; they prized the cowrie shell which must have been transported from the Gulf over long distances: they are found invariably with their backs penetrated, indicating that they were sewn onto clothing as ornaments, a practice common in many societies round the world until very recently. Even the stone material of their tools seems to have been chosen in many instances with an eye to the beauty of the final product.

Travellers in Arabia will frequently see rock faces which have been used until quite recent times to depict images and inscribe writing. Sandstone was the preferred rock, partly because it is relatively easy to work and partly because, on the right rock, the engraving stands out well. A sandstone surface with an iron oxide coating turns dark brown or black with long exposure to the air. By chiselling away this dark surface layer, a fresh yellow or pale brown surface is exposed, which contrasts sharply with the original blackened face and was therefore attractive to the old artists and writers. The passage of time will darken the new surfaces, but they will not revert to the original shade for many hundreds, or perhaps thousands of years. Different sandstones will develop this new patina at different rates depending on the iron content of the stone, but this can be a useful tool in dating these old drawings and graffiti. As a general rule of thumb, the darker the engraving, the older it is.

In many parts of the country no sandstone exists. Basalt and granite are then sometimes used; but these rocks are harder to work, and the end result is less

striking because they have little surface patination. So examples are relatively rare, and figures do not reach the size or exuberance found on sandstone.

The artistic merit of the engravings is in many cases considerable. With an economy of line which the nature of the medium encourages, the artist frequently achieved animation, dignity and other qualities in his drawing; and used the natural contours of the rock to enhance his desired effect.

Besides the pleasure derived from their beauty, the engravings also provide us with a valuable source of knowledge about the dress, customs and weaponry of the contemporary people, and information about the local fauna of the time. A comparison of the drawings shows that they have been executed in a number of different styles, which has allowed scholars to draw up a sequence of changing cultures from the earliest days. The fact that many drawings have been engraved over the top of other, earlier, drawings has also been helpful in assigning relative ages to the different cultures.

A favourite subject of early drawings is cattle, long-horned and with piebald hides. The earliest may represent the wild ox as a beast to be hunted, while later ones appear to celebrate the cow as a domestic animal. Other animals of the hunt which later become common in engravings are ostriches, onagers, ibex, tahr and oryx; while fat-tailed sheep, goats, camels and horses are shown as these animals became domesticated.

The human figures which are depicted in the early neolithic show people with elaborate hairstyles, wearing jewellery or ornamentation round their necks. Clothing is usually represented as carefully made skirts or kilts. Men carry spears, bows and arrows, and boomerangs or killing sticks.

As the neolithic age progressed, climatic conditions became harsher. His rapidly multiplying skills and technology eventually enabled man to cope with

Above: A remarkable frieze of lifesize ostriches high up on a sandstone face. The artist has captured the fast strutting gait of the bird very effectively and used a brilliantly stylised representation for the body.

Top right: The dignified procession of camels on this rock face is the oldest of the engravings. The horsemen the small figures and the script at the top are paler and therefore younger. The central camel appears to be hobbled, which suggsts that these were domesticated.

Above left: A lyre-horned cow and goats represent two of the principal domestic animals of early man. These are drawn with a fine economy of line but are still immediately recognisable. In general, early rock engravings are more skilfully executed than later drawings.

Right: *The mummified body of the 5,300 year old man from the copper age, found in an Alpine glacier. He was armed with a copper axe, a flint dagger and a quiverful of stone-tipped arrows. Many other possessions found scattered in the melting ice around him gave us a precious glimpse of how man in those times lived. He wore a cape of woven fibre, deerskin shoes stuffed with soft grass, a fur cap and other garments. Among his smaller possessions was even a medicinal mushroom on a string. We may assume that his gear was not dissimilar to that of Arabian man at the same time, when the stone age was giving way to the age of copper.*

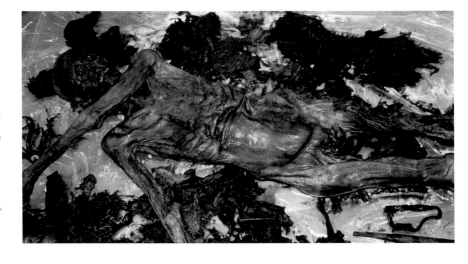

BELOW:

Bottom left: *Broken granite grindstones used to crush ore and slag lie abandoned on an old mine site at al Amar.*

Top left: *Slag, the residue left after smelting, has a distinctive smooth dark appearance.*

Middle: *Miners followed a promising vein of rock deep into a hillside until the vein ran out or the depth made further mining impracticable. This old mine working probably dates from Abbasid times.*

Top right: *Iron pyrites is also known as fool's gold.*

Bottom right: *The green stain of copper reveals the presence of copper ores in the surrounding rock. White and dark grey rock contain gold and zinc.*

the effects of drought more successfully. He had learnt to store grain in stone lined pits; he could travel further and faster, on domesticated animals; and his new weaponry, which now included the bow and arrow, enabled him to hunt much more effectively.

Work is still progressing to establish quite how the stone tool repertoire developed in Arabia in the neolithic age; but it seems likely that the latest development was the introduction of polished stone tools, normally in the form of axe heads. These were not like the handaxes of palaeolithic man, but were much smaller, with a polished smooth edge and designed to be inserted into a haft or handle. Modern experimentation has shown such tools to be extremely effective in felling small trees. They were about the same size as the unusual iron axes carried even today by the Shehu people of the Musandam peninsula, raising an intriguing question about cultural continuity.

When stone tools were finally abandoned in Arabia is not known, but we may surmise that they were gradually replaced by copper, bronze and iron as these metals came into common use. There was probably a long period when both existed

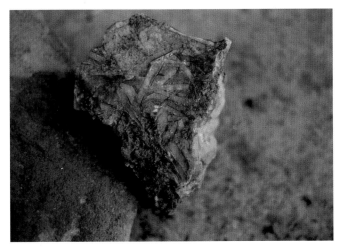

Above: *A specimen of heavy grey sphalerite (zinc ore) and gold-bearing quartz from Al Amar.*

Above left: *Copper and gold deposits are frequently associated with other minerals. At al Amar, for example, jasper, talc and barites (the long white crystals in the photograph) are found associated with the ore body.*

side by side. The "Ice-man" recently discovered thawing out of a glacier in the Alps was found to have been carrying a quiver of arrows tipped with stone, and to have a wooden-handled flint dagger in his belt, but also to have been carrying a well-crafted copper axe. His equipment might well have been typical of Arabia too over a long transitional period. The very first copper was probably being mined in Arabia about 5,000 years ago, but copper objects could have been brought in from the north even before that.

Old mine workings are scattered throughout the Shield area. The shafts and trenches dug out by the miners are still commonly to be seen, as are the heaps of spoil and broken querns, grindstones and stone hammers used to crush the ore. The old miners were producing copper, silver and gold. Frequently these metals were found together and produced from the same mine.

How ancient the first mining in Arabia was is a matter for debate. Timna in Sinai was smelting copper 5,500 years ago, during the late neolithic period, and we may reasonably suppose that mining in Arabia started soon after that. Certainly the bright green copper-bearing mineral, malachite, was as evident on surface rocks in many parts of Arabia as it was at Timna. Throughout antiquity, as metals became important trading commodities, the demand for Arabian metals increased. It is known that metal was still being mined at the time of the revelation of Islam and later in Abbasid times. Probably mining was done more or less continuously from its first origins till then.

From an analysis of the ancient mine workings at Mahd al Dhahab, scientists have calculated that between 750,000 and 1,500,000 ounces of gold may have been produced there. To produce such quantities would have required immense quantities of both charcoal and water. Fortunately for the miners there must have been in their times a wetter climate than there is today; the large quantities of charcoal needed to fire the smelters could only have been provided from forests surrounding the mines, and sufficient water for sluicing was available, if only on a seasonal basis.

Those who have been engaged in the modern search for these metals have ruefully remarked that despite all the massive technology in use to aid their search they have not discovered a single meaningful deposit that had not already been exploited in ancient times. Those early miners were clearly thorough, tenacious and observant. Frequently their eye would have been caught by the white quartz veins in the rock with which gold is often associated, or the bright turquoise of malachite. But much of the richest gold ore, such as that at Al Amar, is dark and the gold contained in it occurs in microscopic particles invisible to the naked eye. How did the ancients recognise it? What first drew them to crush and smelt it? Certainly its occurrence tends to be in association with other conspicuous minerals such as jasper or the dark shiny ore of zinc, or the glitter of chalcopyrites ("fools' gold") but still the mystery remains.

Even before mining began, it is likely that gold was picked out of alluvial deposits in stream beds by panning, or by washing gravel over a fleece so that the heaviest fragments (the gold) would sink fastest and be trapped in the wool. Jason's golden fleece is thought to be a reference to this primitive method of collecting gold.

Several of the more important old gold mines have been re-evaluated by modern mining engineers, and reopened. The best known is Mahd Adh Dhahab (the "cradle of gold") but the mine at Sukhaybirat is also producing gold and Al Amar is in process of being reopened. By using modern recovery methods it is worthwhile to reprocess the waste and tailings from the old mines. Modern surveying techniques and mechanical mining equipment also make accessible extensions to the original ore-body which can be exploited. Mahd Adh Dhahab, for example, is reckoned to be capable of producing over 20 tonnes of gold before becoming exhausted.

While gold was always highly prized for its beauty and decorative value, copper was the first industrial metal exploited for tools, implements, and weapons. Since copper and gold were frequently found in association it may be that they were first produced around the same time. One plausible theory relates their discovery to pottery production. Copper carbonates and sulphides in the forms of turquoise, malachite and azurite were used in powdered form to decorate early ceramics. Some of these pigments may have deformed as strips of bright metallic copper in the kiln; curiosity and experiment could then have led on to the smelting of these minerals in the kilns originally built to fire pottery. What is certain is that the metal could not have been as is frequently assumed produced accidentally from firestones surrounding a campfire. For one thing the temperatures required for smelting ore (800 degrees C) are far higher than could be obtained by such accidental means.

Copper is an effective material for making tools and weapons but suffers from the disadvantage of being rather soft. When tin is added to copper the resulting alloy, bronze, is very much more durable. The first record of bronze manufacture is around 5,000 years ago in Assyria, Iran and Turkey. For 2,500 years until the introduction of iron it was the metal on which civilisation was built: weapons, agricultural tools, household utensils and ornaments were all made for preference from bronze. Tin is much rarer than copper; it is known to have been obtained from the Taurus Mountains of Turkey and from Afghanistan, but so far no direct evidence of ancient tin-mining in Arabia is known. There are some old mine workings at Silsilah in the northeast of the Shield, west of Buraidah, but these seem to have been trial pits dug by miners looking for gold deposits. Arabian bronze was probably imported from the countries to the north, which had by that time a well-developed trading network in place.

Other minerals were also exploited. There is in the area around Dawadmi, 300 kilometres west of Riyadh on the old Makkah road, a whole series of ancient mine workings. These trenches, spoil heaps and buildings were left behind by miners of the Abbasid period who worked the area between 800 and 1200 years ago. This was a time when gold was also exploited in the Shield, and coincided with the construction and heavy use of the Darb Zubaydah, the pilgrim route to Makkah from the Abbasid capital of Baghdad. The miners were exploiting the silver which occurs throughout the district in a radius of 15 kilometres from Dawadmi, usually associated with quartz veins in the predominant granite rocks of the region. Some veins were followed down more than 50 metres below ground level, and several of the trenches are hundreds of metres long, showing that the metal was in economically justifiable quantities at the time. Approximately 100 occurences of silver have been located in the district, all of them unfortunately now too small to justify production at today's prevailing prices.

Not only metals were mined. There is evidence of ancient working of talc deposits near Umm Lajj on the Red Sea coast. Talc is a soft mineral with a soapy texture which has many industrial uses, including use as a ceramic additive and as a filler in paper manufacture, apart from its better-known cosmetic function. Deposits are not uncommon in the Shield, and are sometimes associated with gold occurrences, as at Al Amar where the substantial deposits may be economically viable. In the old days it was mined for carving into cooking pots, ornamental objects and other such things: it was easy to work and withstood the heat of a fire. The craft of working with this material is still pursued in the Asir; the suq in Abha has well-made pots of steatite, a variety of talc.

Since Neolithic times, water has been a scarce and precious commodity in Saudi Arabia. From the time the abundant rains began to fail 4,500 years ago it

Above: *A modern steatite cooking pot from Abha. The craft has been revived and results in good-looking and functional ware.*

Left: *Hand dug wells reached down into the water-bearing gravel in wadi beds, from where the water was brought by animal power to the surface by rope and pulley. This well is at Dir'iyyah in Wadi Hanifah.*

Right: *This dam once trapped water in a tributary of Wadi Laban. Most of the old dams in Arabia lie further west, in the hills of the Hejaz.*

has been in progressively shorter supply.

There are very few naturally occurring sources of perennial water. A number of springs in the western mountains flow throughout the year, feeding streams which flow for a limited distance. On the eastern side of the country the few great oases in Qatif, Al Ahsa and Yabrin have traditionally been fed by artesian springs bubbling up from the limestone rock. In the centre, a few scattered sink-holes in the districts of Al Kharj and Layla have provided constant water, as have sporadic dahls, or natural wells, in the karst limestone of the Summan. The rest of the country was largely devoid of naturally occurring water sources other than those provided by the sparse seasonal rainfall.

And yet, despite the dry surface of the land, there is water in abundance in many parts of the Kingdom, underground. Some of this is the residue of recent rainfall, lying under wadi beds in the alluvial gravels and soils. The rest is older. Many of the sedimentary strata surrounding the Shield are porous, and over the centuries have become saturated with water percolating slowly down from the surface and along the lie of the strata. Man had to win this water with hard work by constructing dams or digging, by hand, shallow wells which were jealously guarded, since life depended on the uninterrupted flow of pure water from them. Contamination and over-consumption were scrupulously avoided.

With the advent of agriculture and settled life in late Neolithic times it became worthwhile to invest considerable resources of time and effort in taming and controlling the water supply. Each geographic area presented its own problems, and the solutions devised were equally various and ingenious.

In the west, the mountainous terrain and high but fiercely concentrated annual rainfall made erosion control and water storage the important matters to control. From Yemen north to Taif it is common to see ancient terraces of dry-stone walling, one above the other. These reduced the runoff of the rains and allowed moisture to be retained in the soil, for the benefit of the terrace agriculture. The flat terrace surfaces also made it easier to direct irrigated water stored

Left: *Looking into the deep dry pit of one of the smaller Uyun near Layla, now completely dry as the shallow aquifer has been fully exploited. The inset photograph shows how the same pit looked 20 years ago.*

behind dams higher up on the slopes to the places where it was needed. Some of these dams are masterpieces of early engineering, and remain substantially intact today, more than two thousand years later, though the majority have now been breached in the centre. Their purpose was to trap some of the flash flood-water and make it available to irrigate the lower fields during dry periods of the growing season through a system of sluices and channels. The dams are faced with masonry on both sides, and taper towards the top. Many of them still show remnants of the original plaster or mortar coating on the upstream side; this would have been applied to reduce the leakage of water through the drystone dam. The greatest of these dams was at Marib in the Yemen. In Saudi Arabia fine examples can be seen in the wadis near Taif, and near Khaybar north of Madina. Many date from before the advent of Islam. There are also a few good but later examples in Najd; one can be seen 20 kilometres west of Riyadh just off the Makkah road. The dam at Rawdat Sudair, 100 kilometres north of Riyadh on the old Qassim road, is also remarkable for its length, fineness of construction, and interesting design.

The Saudi Ministry of Agriculture and Water in recent years has built hundreds of dams and barrages across many of the principal wadis in the Kingdom. These are rather different in purpose from the ancient dams, in that they do not function as reservoirs from which to draw irrigation water directly; instead, they are designed to trap flood water temporarily so that it sinks into the gravel or alluvium bed of the wadi behind the dam, then percolates downstream through the wadi deposits, so recharging the aquifer. These dams are so designed that there is no impediment to water flow in the subsurface gravels. They also prevent soil erosion and damage to farms and property lower down the valley, and allow a wider area to be cultivated than was possible before their construction. Some are very large, such as the Najran dam built in the late 1970s, or the new dam at Bisha which has a storage capacity of 325 million cubic metres, and is one of more than 50 built in Asir Province alone during recent years.

In Central Province is the Saudi Kingdom's best example of a different response to a water control problem, the problem in this case being how to irrigate an area of flat ground some metres above the natural water level. Between the towns of Layla and Badie on the road south from Riyadh towards Sulayyil lie the Uyun, a chain of deep sink holes. The largest of these contains a lake, now some 30 metres below the level of the surrounding ground. For many miles around there are surface deposits of gypsum, proving the existence 20,000 years ago of a vast lake covering an area of over 150 square kilometres. This lake was contemporary with other substantial lakes in Al Ahsa, Yabrin, Mundafan and elsewhere which reached their maximum extent during that wet period in the country's history. The Layla lake gradually shrank until in early historical times, when man first began to use its waters to irrigate farmland, it had reduced in area to about two square kilometres, still a sizeable body of water.

Over the last two thousand years it retreated further until it occupied only the 17 small deep lakes which constituted the Uyun until the 1980s. These deep lakes filled sink holes in the limestone terrain, caused by the same phenomenon which created Ain Hit, the Kharj pit, and the pit at Khafs Daghrah between Kharj and Layla. The anhydrite layer underlying the limestone was dissolved away by groundwater action, leaving caverns deep underground: as these caverns expanded in size the rock strata above simply collapsed into the void thus created, and a sink-hole was formed.

Most of the smaller lakes are now dry, but the main lake, known as Arras, still contains water, though its surface level has dropped considerably over the last two decades. As agriculture and the neighbouring towns have developed, taking water from the surrounding shallow aquifer, the aquifer level has declined in the area; the lakes act as a gauge for the general fall in the water level.

The traditional system of irrigation in Layla, the *qanat* or *falaj* (in Omani terminology), was that commonly used around the Arabian Gulf. It is used extensively in Iran, Oman, and Iraq, and also in the oasis of Al Ahsa in Eastern Province. A *qanat* is essentially a subterranean canal. Starting from a reliable

Above: A carefully graded tunnel, or qanat, *below ground carried water from the Layla lakes to irrigated land. The circular structures are shafts originally opened for removing spoil during construction of the tunnel and preserved for maintenance operations. With the drying of the Uyun, the* qanat *fell into disuse.*

Right: A timeless scene in the al Ahsa oasis. For thousands of years the date palm has been cultivated here on the same ground, using water welling up naturally from the aquifers.

water source a tunnel is excavated to the area required to be irrigated. Every 20 or 30 metres along its length a hole is made to the surface to permit the excavation of spoil during its construction and allow for maintenance once in operation. These manholes reveal the course of the *qanat*. Some *qanats* are several kilometres in length, falling in a very slight gradient from the water source.

In Layla the *qanats* are now only of historical interest, for the level of the original water source has fallen too far for them to be useful. But when they were first constructed the water level, then about two metres below ground level, must have seemed immutable. A well can be dug down, if the water level drops, until the new level is found; not so for *qanats*, which lose their utility completely if the water source fails or drops below the original level. Today, using modern drilling technology and modern piping and pumping equipment, water can be obtained for towns and farms with relative ease, but the ingenuity and immense labour of the old farmers still evoke admiration.

Further east, naturally occurring water is concentrated in a few localities which constitute the largest oases in the Kingdom. Along the coast north of Dammam are Sayhat, Qatif and Tarut, all with old and extensive date groves and other types of farming. Inland at Al Ahsa and Yabrin are two other great oases, though Yabrin's salty soil makes it difficult to derive as much benefit as would otherwise be the case from the millions of cubic metres estimated to well through the subsoil and evaporate each year.

These eastern oases have been inhabited continuously for many thousands of years. Pottery and other relics of the Ubaid culture, predating the civilisations of ancient Sumer and Akkad, have turned up in this area, together with evidence of many other civilisations since then. Bahrain, too, can be classed with these oases; the water which supplies them all is from the same source, the Dammam and Neogene aquifers.

One of the wonders of the Arabian Gulf is the occurrence of fresh water in the midst of the salt sea. Ain Mizahim, one kilometre offshore from Al Khobar, and the Ghumisa spring five kilometres offshore and ten kilometres north of Jubail, are famous examples.

There used even to be a freshwater spring in Dammam harbour until it was blocked by dredging operations during the expansion of the port. To be able to collect fresh water from the sea was a boon for old-time fishermen and pearlers. These springs also derived from the same aquifer sources.

By far the most prolific group of these artesian springs is in Al Ahsa, which is in turn and as a consequence the greatest oasis in Saudi Arabia. It lies on the eastern edge of the Shedgum Plateau, an outlier of the Summan, where a low cliff falls away to an extensive depression. Hofuf, the main town, and upwards of forty other smaller towns and villages are supported by many miles of intensive agriculture, including millions of palm trees of different varieties, particularly the local favourite, the Ikhlas. The oasis has been inhabited since the earliest times and has always been an important centre. The Al Jawatha mosque, third oldest in Islam, still attracts worshippers. The fact that it should have been the first place outside the two holy places to have built a mosque testifies to its importance even then. Before the advent of Islam it had been a focus for earlier civilisations: successive remains from the stone age, from the Ubaid culture and Hellenistic times testify to its enduring importance.

The source of Hofuf's prosperity is the artesian water which comes to the surface in over a hundred springs in the oasis. This is fossil water, surfacing at a temperature of 36 degrees Centigrade. The traditional method of employing the water was to divert some for domestic purposes from the head of the spring, sometimes having it flow through bath-houses and wash-houses before leading it through innumerable irrigation channels to water the cultivated land. From there it flowed into one of the *sabkha* lakebeds which lie in a rough crescent shape from northeast round to southeast of the oasis. These *sabkhas* are the site of earlier extensive freshwater lakes. Some 20,000 years ago the artesian springs flowed at a greater rate and were supplemented by much higher rainfall than today. The combination resulted in the creation of these lakes, which persisted until quite recent times. The last of them was drained only this century. The outflow from the lakes ran north and then east in a river, 100 feet across as it left the lake, which flowed perennially into the Gulf. All the early geographers such as Ptolemy, Yaqut and al Idrisi showed this river on their maps of the Gulf. But from the 13th century A.D. onwards respectable geographers failed to show it. The reason is that its course was blocked at about that time by the southward movement of the mobile Jafurah sands, and the decreasing rate of flow (the lakes were declining in size by that time) was insufficient to clear the invading sands from the river's channel. Nonetheless, the outflow still persists today, not as a continuous river but as slower, partly subterranean drainage along the old route. It is in this area that the famous undiscovered ancient city of Gerrha must lie, perhaps covered by the Jafurah sands, unless as one modern theory supposes Gerrha is simply a mis-transcription of Hajara, the old name for Hofuf, in which case the ruins will one day be discovered within the bounds of the oasis.

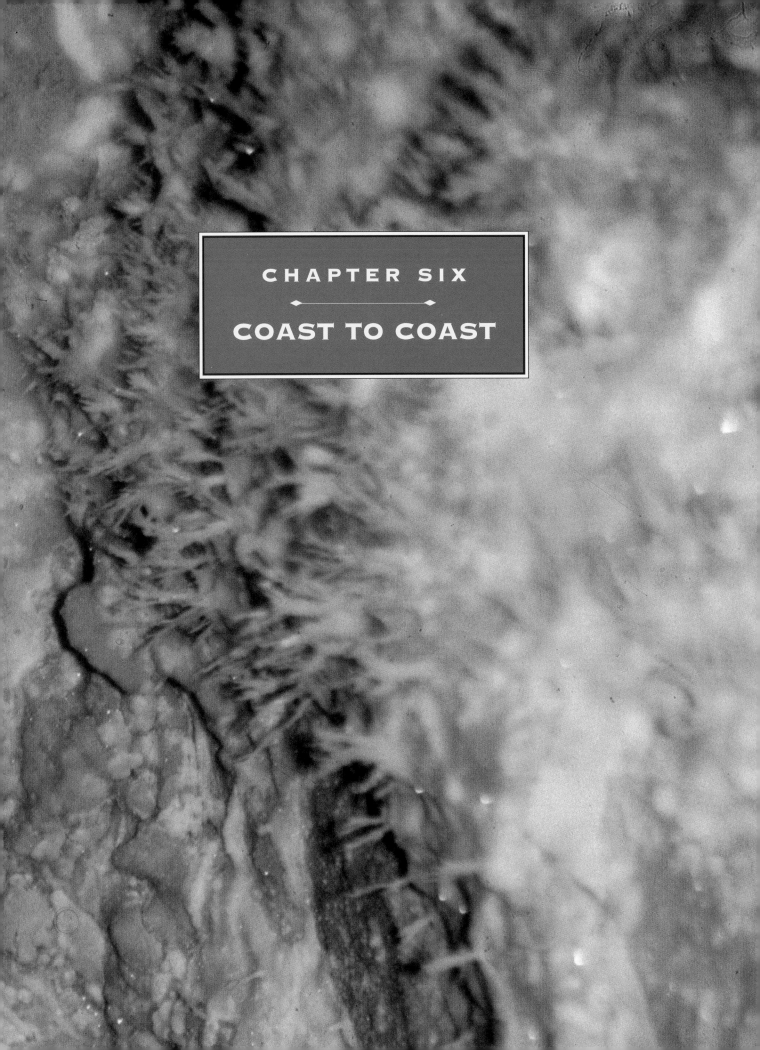

CHAPTER SIX

COAST TO COAST

The shoreline of the Arabian Gulf is for most of its length low-lying; loose soft sand undulates inland, the height of its low ridges scarcely above the level of the salt marshes which lie between them. The marshes are treacherous; they have a hard salt crust in dry weather but underneath they remain a salty mush in which animals and vehicles can be irretrievably lost if they break through the crust.

These salt marshes, or *sabkhas*, are areas where evaporite rocks are forming today. The water in them is constantly being lost by evaporation, the salts remaining behind. The water comes from rain, from the underground discharge of fresh water aquifers and, near the coast, from sea water percolating inland. The most extensive *sabkha* to be seen easily today is the Sabkhat Matti, southeast of Qatar; 3,000 square kilometres in extent, it is a barren salt flat, so low-lying that even 100 kilometres inland from its northern edge on the Gulf it is still less than 50 metres above sea level.

Inland from the featureless and flat coastal belt the eye is caught by a low east-facing cliff and isolated steep jebels around the Al Ahsa oasis. These are the eastern edge of the Summan plateau. The cliff faces represent a previous Gulf coastline. The abrasive action of the waves on the Pliocene shore deeply undercut the soft rock, producing cliffs and, in Jebel Qara in the oasis, caves cutting into the heart of the jebel, now a much-visited tourist destination.

Above the escarpment the land stretches for 300 kilometres to the northwest in a generally featureless low plateau. The Miocene sedimentary rocks under-

Below: *A wet spring day shows the edge of the Summan escarpment, cut away by waves in Pliocene times, when the waters of the Gulf reached inland to the Hofuf area.*

foot gradually change from marine to non-marine as you pass over the limits of one of the old sea invasions. On the first part of the journey marine fossils molluscs, sharks' teeth and others are locally plentiful on the soft crumbling surface; further west the surface changes to duricrust, a hard cemented limestone conglomerate or breccia. This duricrust is a thin skin on the surface of the land, and conceals a soft and porous limestone below which is riddled with tunnels and caves. This extraordinary underground landscape would not be guessed at by a traveller. The only indications that it exists at all are infrequent small holes in the surface, known as *dahls*, which give access for the intrepid to the caves and passages below.

The most attractive feature of parts of the Summan is the occasional *rawdat* which relieves the bleak surface. The Arabic word *rawdat* (the plural of which is *riyadh*) means garden, or meadow. The plateau gives way suddenly to broad circular sinkholes or depressions filled with trees and bushes, deep enough below the plateau surface for the tops of the trees barely to show above the horizon as you approach. The depressions have accumulated a layer of silt in their bottoms, which enables the trees and larger bushes to root themselves better than the inhospitable duricrust of the surrounding plain allows. In spring they are some of the most delightful places in Arabia, with rainwater pools, grass and flowers.

South from the Summan the old Darb Al Kuwait track still runs to the town of Rumah down over the gently rolling Dahna sands, their dunes in parallel lines

Below, below right: Strange rock formations, cliffs and caves make the Jebel Qara in al Ahsa a popular resort. The rock is soft and easily weathered; the apparently darker top is an effect produced by rain.

DAHLS

Rainwater interacts with carbon dioxide in soil to produce small amounts of carbonic acid, which percolates into the ground with the rainwater. Seeping down through cracks and joints in the bedrock, the carbonic acid slowly dissolves the limestone and carries it away in solution, widening the cracks and creating larger cavities and caves. In the Summan area are numerous "dahls", or vertical holes in the limestone floor of the desert. Some of these go down to the water table and have been used as natural wells since time immemorial, as evidenced by the grooves worn in the rock at the edge of the holes by the ropes used to haul the water buckets to the surface. Most "dahls", though, are dry, and were formed when the roof of an underground cavern collapsed. The cave systems here, most notably in the area around Maaqala, are of variable length, sometimes running several hundreds of metres horizontally.

The hard duricrust of the surface in much of this region conceals the porous nature of the underlying limestone. Where it is accessible from a dahl, the subsurface is seen to be riddled with tunnels and passages at a depth of 5 to 10 metres; many of these are blocked with wind blown sand, which tends to drift into the dahl entrances In some Summan caves the walls and roofs are covered with crystals, which can only have been formed in water, showing that the dissolution process happened when the land was covered by sea or when the water table was much higher than it is today. Similar evidence comes from the smooth calcite layer coating the walls and roofs of some of the limestone tunnels, which would have been deposited by a mineral-charged flow of water over a long timespan.

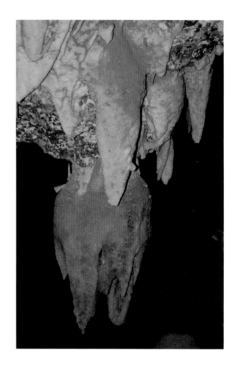

Below: *Cross-section of the subsurface in a karst area. Under the hard surface, the land is criss-crossed with trunnels. Since the rock is soft, roof collapses are common, so passages tend not to be level. At deeper levels water may be found.*

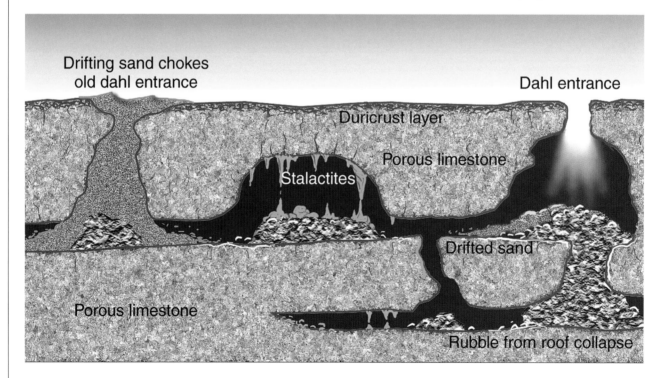

Drifting sand chokes old dahl entrance

Dahl entrance

Duricrust layer

Porous limestone

Stalactites

Drifted sand

Porous limestone

Rubble from roof collapse

After the caves were formed and the water table fell, water charged with dissolved calcium carbonate continued to drip through the duricrust roof and walls. As the carbon dioxide in the water was lost the calcium carbonate precipitated to form helictites, stalactites, stalagmites, flowstone and other curious and beautiful formations. In today's arid climate most of these formations are no longer growing, but some caves remain humid and show evidence of "live" formations: the stalactites still drip, and the flowstone surfaces gleam with moisture.

Above: *The roofs of some caves sparkle with crystals; others are crusted with helictites such as these, a form of small stalactites which appears at first sight to be a form of plant life.*

Above left: *The rather featureless surface of much of the Summan conceals a surprising underground world. Sparse entrances, usually much smaller than the one photographed, give access to labyrinths of caves and tunnels. Careless visitors can damage the fragile and beautiful formations underground.*

Left, top left: *Not all stalactites are simple pointed columns. They can take many varied and unusual forms, such as these in Dahl Sultan.*

Right: *Both views look along the line of the Tuwaiq escarpment. Less than half the height of the escarpment is exposed as a cliff face. The rest is a deep talus or scree slope which is slowly being washed out by erosion.*

oriented NW-SE. Twenty kilometres out of Rumah on the road to Riyadh, now in limestone country, you cross from Tertiary to Cretaceous rock, from the age of mammals back into the age of dinosaurs. On the far side is the world prior to the great Cretaceous extinction. From here to Riyadh, and from Riyadh on down the Makkah road to the Shield at Quwayiyah, you are going back in time; you are also going uphill. Since you descend a number of escarpments on the way it is hard to realise this; it seems as if you must be descending. But between each escarpment the land rises at a very slight gradient, and more than sufficient overall to compensate for the escarpment descents. The land between the escarpments is mostly filled with erosion debris from the escarpment faces but the escarpments themselves give a cross-section of the whole of the Mesozoic era, 180 million years.

The most spectacular and highest of the escarpments is the Jebel Tuwaiq. Where the main road cuts through, it consists throughout its height of marine limestone, except for a few thin layers of grey shale. The cliff face of the Tuwaiq exposes different rocks further north and south. Eighty kilometres to the south the lower half is Minjur sandstone, with Marrat and Dhurma limestone on the upper slopes. As you climb the face of the cliff, for example to the splendid viewpoint on top of the outlying Jebel Baloum, it is quite obvious how both the stone and the fossil fauna change.

Left: *At the interface between the Shield and the later sedimentary rocks, limestone rests on rugged dark igneous rocks.*

Where the last of the Mesozoic sedimentary rocks ends, 100 kilometres west of the Tuwaiq escarpment, a line of dark hills appears on the western horizon. It is clear even at a distance that these are quite different from anything seen since leaving the Gulf coast. All the horizons so far have been flat, horizontal, pale. These hills are dark: dark gray, dark green, black. They also have a jagged edge, a tumbled, pointed appearance. This is the Shield. As you go west through Quwayiyah the last horizontal line, where the Permian Khuff formation laps onto the black Shield, comes to an end.

The new landscape has its own beauty. The wild rocks with their fantastic shapes and dark colours have great visual appeal, offset against the gritty white quartz sand in the valleys between them.

Left: *Mirage distorts the hills at the eastern edge of the Shield.*

Further still to the west, the belt of *harrats* extends up the east side of the mountain watershed. Uniformly black, they present the most desolate landscape in Arabia, which is saying something. Tracks through them are few and stony. The *harrats* are made of basalt, and since they are of recent origin are relatively unweathered. In some places they look like frozen treacle; in others, where wadis have cut through them, they look like columns or palisades. Other fantastic features are long tunnels formed like a protective skin by streams of molten basalt: as the outer part of the lava stream cooled into rock the inner part of the flow, protected from cooling by the rock tunnel, continued flowing and repeated the process until the eruption ended and the last of the lava flowed out of the tunnel.

The crater at Wahbah in the Harrat al Kishb appears to have formed when an

Left: *The Wahbah crater, ringed with cliffs. One gully breaching the cliffs allows access to the crater floor.*

explosive eruption occurred, scattering rock for miles around and leaving behind an impressive crater. Among the rock debris on the crater rim are small green peridots and shiny lumps of volcanic glass, called obsidian.

Many extinct volcanoes lie in the *harrats*. Most are hard to get to, but offer remarkable views from the summits: down into the crater, now often with a skin of white salts at the crater bottom, and out across the black volcano-studded *harrat*. On the way, you will pass lumps of pumice, volcanic ash, "bombs" of lava thrown high out of the craters and rapidly cooled so that they look like loaves of crusty bread, and shining obsidian.

In the northwest, between Al Ula and Tabuk the *harrats* flow to and over the edge of high Cambrian and Ordovician sandstone escarpments, and enhance an already very beautiful landscape with a sudden juxtaposition of black and yellow; a sharp contrast to the granite and schist underlying the most southerly harrat in Saudi Arabia, the Harrat Buqum, which runs parallel to and east of the road from Taif to Al Baha.

Right: *Wadi Qaraqir's dramatic sandstone scenery hides narrow green canyons. Here a doum palm grows wild; elsewhere dates and other crops are cultivated.*

Above: *A smooth granite whaleback rises out of the gravel plain. Etched on the skyline a series of boulders balance precariously on the slope.*

Left, below: *The rising sun lights up a typical granite boulder mass. Weathering rounds off the boulder tops and excavates hollows on the underside of the rocks.*

Leaving the *harrat* country behind, the road from Al Baha to Abha is arguably the most scenic in Arabia. It combines fine mountain views and vertiginous prospects west down towards the distant Tihama plain with picturesque juniper woods and pockets of domestic greenery. The nature of the terrain changes as you go south, because of the basic change in the underlying rock. Soon after leaving Al Baha, an area of metamorphic schist, the road crosses an area of granite country for fifty kilometres, with spectacular smooth faces and rounded boulders of granite, before again changing abruptly to greenstone for the last fifty kilometres to Abha. Now the rocks are rougher, darker; the hills are more pointed and jagged. All along the road the best places to examine specimens of the rocks are in the roadcuts, where fresh faces have been cut into the rock during road-building operations.

From Abha the road plunges down the Wadi ad Dila towards the Tihamah plain. The main wadi and its tributary wadis are all in the V-shape typical of erosion on steep crystalline slopes.Perhaps the most dramatic evidence of the power of erosion in this area is in the ruins of a large concrete bridge which used to carry the road across the wadi but which now lies in ruins a considerable distance downstream, in sections weighing many hundreds of tons each, heavily pock-marked where boulders in the torrent have smashed the face of the concrete.

As the road descends its angle eases and it emerges from the defile. In front is the Tihama, its sandy surface concealing far beneath great blocks of the Shield which were down-faulted when this rift valley opened, and concealing also the later limestone sediments and the depths of gravel swept off the mountains behind. As you near the coast, crossing remains of old limestone reefs, the ground turns into *sabkha*, like the salt-marshes on the Gulf shore, and dips under the vivid living corals of the Red Sea, tomorrow's rock.

Overleaf: From the shore of the Red Sea near Al Wejh, the jagged outline of the Shield is silhouetted by sunset.

INDEX

SELECT BIBLIOGRAPHY

Anati E., *Rock Art in Central Arabia.* Louvain, 1973

ATLAL, *The Journal of Saudi Arabian Archaeology*, Riyadh.

Bordaz J. *Tools of the Old and New Stone Age*, David & Charles.

Camp V.E. & Roobol J., *Evolution of Harrat Rahat*, GSAB, 1989
                          Evolution of Harrats Khaybat Ithnayn & Kura, GSAB, 1991.

Clarke M.H., *Oman's Geological Heritage*, Petroleum Development Oman, 1990.

Cloudlsey-Thompson J.L., *Desert Life*, Pergamon Press, 1965.

Collonette P & Grainger D.J., *Midneral Resources of Saudi Arabia*, DGMR, Jeddah 1994.

Department of Antiquities & Museums, Riyadh, *An Introduction to Saudi Arabian Antiquities, 1975.*

Dixon D., *The Practical Geologist*, Simon & Schuster, 1992.

Facey W., *The Eastern Province of Saudi Arabia*, Stacey International, 1994.

Gould S.J., *Wonderful Life*, Hutchinson Radius, 1989.

Khan M., *Prehistoric Rock Art of Northern Saudi Arabia*, Department of Antiquities, Riyadh, 1993

King Saud University, Riyadh, *Pre-Islamic Arabia*, 1984.

Larsen C.E., *Life and Land Use on the Bahrain Islands*, Chicago, 1983.

Maddin R. (ed.), *The Beginning of the Use of Metals & Alloys*, MIT, 1986.

McClure H.A., *Permian-Carboniferous Glaciation in the Arabian Peninsula*, GSAB 1980.

McPhee J., *Basin and Range*, Noonday, 1991.

Nayeem M.A., *Prehistory and Protohistory of the Arabian Peninsula*, Hyderabad, 1990.

Oakley K.P., *Man the Tool-Maker*, British Museum, 1972.

Pallister J.S., *Magmatic History of Red Sea Rifting*, GSAB, 1987.

Powers, Ramirez, Redmond & Elberg, *Geology of the Arabian Peninsula*, USGS, 1966.

Reader J., *Missing Links*, Penguin, 1990.

Ross & Schlee, *Shallow Structure and Geological Development of the Southern Red Sea*, GSAB, 1973.

Sayari S. & Zotl , *The Quaternary Period in Saudi Arabia*, Springer Verlag, 1978.

Schick K.D. & Toth N, *Making Silent Stones Speak*, Weidenfeld & Nicolson, 1993.

Skinner B.J. & Porter S.C., *Physical Geology*, Wiley, 1978.

Spencer C., *Mineral Wealth of Saudi Arabia*, Immel, 1986.

Spoczynska J. O. I., *Fossils – a Study in Evolution*, Muller, 1971.

Stoeser D.B. & Camp V.E., *Pan-African microplate accretion to the Arabian Shield*, GSAB, 1985

Swinnerton H.H., *Fossils*, Collins, 1989.

Wilson E.O., *The Diversity of Life*, Penguin, 1992.

Abbreviations

| GSAB | Geological Society of America Bulletin |
| USGA | United States Geological Survey |